A Book of Uncommon Prayer

100 Celebrations of the Miracle & Muddle of the Ordinary

Brian Doyle

SORIN BOOKS  Notre Dame, Indiana www.sorinbooks.com

Paperback: ISBN-13 978-1-933495-62-0

E-Book: ISBN-13 978-1-933495-63-7

Cover image © KriulinV / Thinkstock.com.

Cover and text design by Andy Wagoner.

Printed and bound in the United States of America.

Library of Congress Cataloging-in-Publication Data

Doyle, Brian, 1956 November 6-

  A book of uncommon prayer : 100 celebrations of the miracle & muddle of the ordinary / Brian Doyle.

    pages cm

  Includes bibliographical references and index.

  ISBN 978-1-933495-62-0 (alk. paper) -- ISBN 1-933495-62-6 (alk. paper)

  1. Prayers. I. Title.

  BV260.D69 2014

  242'.8--dc23

                          2014036641

To my sister Elisabeta,
now Ani Dechi Palmo,
of Kagyu Thubten Chöling
Monastery in New York,
with my love and gratitude
for your kindness & grace

Hey Cath,

I feel like Doyle
has summarized here
most of our
conversations :)

Love,

Jill

Contents

Prayer for the Idiot Author That He Doesn't Totally Punt in the Pages That Follow

---

Because, o Lord, he *has* punted, o my yes, more times than he can remember, and he is memorious by nature, and remembers many booming punts all too vividly, for example endless shades of lies and prevarications with young ladies, and the occasional mixing of fiction and fact in reportage, and flares and bursts of temper, and the selfish insistence on his way in various familial and marital disputes, and the lack of excellent listening skills sometimes, and sloth, and lust, although not gluttony or envy and not much pride, technically, although my good showing with these three might be more a function of age than a stalwart character or growth of spirit. Still, though, the lifetime punting . . . well, let's not go into it. Suffice it to say that I pray that in the pages that follow I will be able to catch and speak something true and honest and genuine and blunt about seeing and celebrating and savoring the slather of Your gifts upon me and us; and will be able to sing, even creakily and croakingly, of the holiness everywhere evident and available; and will be able to remind readers that we are handed miracles beyond number, every blessed moment, if only we can train ourselves to open and see and hear and taste and feel and smell and absorb them, and so be blessed ever deeper by Your mercy and profligate generosity and wry subtle humor. This I pray most humbly, while trying not to think of—o God help me—a thousand tremendous soaring epic punts in the past. And so: amen.

Brian Doyle

Prayer for the Kindergarten Boy Who Asked Me, *How Do You Manage to Get So Many Words on a Single Page of Your Book, Mister?*

First of all I thought my head was going to fly off with joy, and then I had to resist the urge to bend down and hug this kid so hard his eyes would gog out, and then I had to explain to him and his classmates how I write books, which is that I write really big sentences and then a tiny lady inside my computer converts them to little lines that will fit on the pages of printed books, and then I had to explain that I was just kidding, and then my hour in their classroom drew to a close, and they signed autographs for me, and I signed one child's hand, to general merriment, and then we took a class picture and I got them to pretend to pick their noses just before the teacher took our photograph, which we all thought was funny but she didn't, and then I drove home. But on the way home I thought for the one-millionth time that I am the luckiest man ever because the Breath Who Dreamed Everything into Being gave me three children of my own, and many thousands of children of my own who came from people other than my lovely bride, and not for the first time and not for the last I concluded that little kids are the coolest things in the whole world, even better than beer and sneakers and osprey. And so: amen.

Prayer for Cashiers and Checkout-Counter Folks

Who endure the cold swirls of winter from the sliding doors that are opening and closing every forty seconds; and who endure pomposity and buffoonery and minor madness in their customers; and who gently help the shuffling old lady in the ancient camel coat count out the right change for her loaf of bread and single sad can of cat food; and cheerfully also disburse stamps and cash along with bagging the groceries and even occasionally carting them out swiftly for the customers they know are frail and wobbly; and who must sometimes silently want to scream and shriek in weariness and wondering how it is that they are here for eight hours at a stretch; and who do their jobs with patience and diligence, knowing the price of every single blessed thing in the store; and who ask after children and the ill among the families of their customers with honest interest and concern; and who gently refuse to sell beer to teenagers but do not make a big deal out of it and ring the manager; and who seem to me generally paragons of grace in situations where it would be so easy to grow sad and exhausted and bored; so we ask Your blessing upon them, in their millions around the world; and we ask that You choose a moment at Your discretion, and reach for all of them at once in Your unimaginable way, and jazz them with hope and laughter, and give them a dollop of Your starlight, so that they will, for an instant, feel a surge of joy, for reasons they do not know; but we do. And so: amen.

Prayer in Thanks for Decent Shoes

Do we take them for granted? Of course we take them for granted. We don them, slip them on, shuffle into them, doff them, toss them, kick them to the back of the closet, and never not once do we say, o Coherent Mercy, thank You for the skins and wood and cloth that keepeth our feet from the flinty earth, that swaddleth our flippers and protecteth our toes, that allow us to wander about briskly without (a) tearing the pads of our feet to shreds in thorny bristle and granite dagger and (b) losing various toes to steamrollers and arrogant bicyclists and testy rattlesnakes and spinning cricket bats and such.

Did we stop for a moment, this morning, in the silvery light of dawn, and stare at our silent battered footboats, and think of the poor bovine whose skin this is, of the quiet woman who cut and hammered and built them, of the man who carted them from the place of their shaping to the spot of their sale, of the lanky boy who bent from his great height to affix them to our ancient feet, and measure the comfort of that fit, and note cheerfully that they were actually on sale this week, sir, did you know?

No, we did not. But we should pause, here and there, for these small things, for they are not at all small, as we know. The cow was once alive, and so it was holy, alive with the Breath; the woman and the man and the boy alive, and so holy, children of the Breath; their sacrifice and their labor a gift and a prayer, songs of the Breath; their marshaling of skills and gifts to in good work a prayer also, a song to and with the Breath; for that is why we are here, is that not so? To discover what it is we do well, and then hone and shape and wield those gifts, in the making and doing of things cleanly and creatively, without ego and bluster and flutter and boast, in companionable service to our fellow beings? Is that not so? And is not the evidence of that effort everywhere, even and especially, this morning, perceptible at the tapered ends of our legs? And so: amen.

Prayer for Robert Louis Stevenson on His Birthday, November 13

Because he was a lonely only child who as he matured learned to use his incredible storytelling gifts to make stories read by millions of children around the world, to their immense delight; and many of those children were lonely too, and found a refuge and a pleasure and a respite and a joy in his books that seem holy to me. Because he thrashed around being selfish and reckless when he was young and then marshaled and channeled himself and became a man of legendary kindness and courtesy and generosity and empathy and humor, which is what we all want to grow up to be, don't we? Because he was, according to his stepdaughter and stepson, the greatest second dad ever, which must be a difficult and confusing and painful job, which he did well. Because when he matured as a writer he stopped commenting and lecturing and sermonizing and homilizing, which made his work ever so much more enlightening and edifying and moving and extraordinary. Because he punctured the fastuous and the pompous and the arrogant whenever and wherever he saw it, with rare skill and passion. Because he was by all accounts a terrific husband to a wife who could be obstreperous and testy and selfish and unempathetic and hard of hearing to her husband's dreams, but never for a day, by her own account, was he less than tender and open to her. Because he saw long before other visitors to the South Seas that the incursion of money and bullets and liquor would destroy the cultures that had grown up there over a thousand years, and were in many ways wise and healthy. Because he invented a new prayer every night at dinner at his family's table in the jungled hills of Samoa, and they prayed together aloud for peace and joy and the strength to bring light against the darkness; which he did, as well as any man who ever set pen to paper, and so it is that this day every year we pause, and thank You for the gift of that lean amused Scotchman, and bow in gratitude for his wit and energy and huge heart, which blessed the world in ways we can never measure; but we can celebrate and appreciate them today and every day. And so: amen.

Prayer in Celebration of the Greatest Invention Ever, the Wicked Hot Shower

O God help me bless my soul is there any pleasure quite so artless and glorious and simple and unadorned and productive and restorative as a blazing hot shower when you really *really* want a hot shower? When you are not yet fully awake, when you are wiped from two hours of serious basketball, when you are weary and speechless after trip or trauma? Thank You, Inventiveness, for making a universe where there is water, and heat, and nozzles, and towels, and steam, and hairbrushes, and razors for cutting that line that distinguishes your beard from your chest, and toothbrushes. Thank You most of all, Generosity, for water. Deft invention, water. Who would have ever thought to mix hydrogen and oxygen so profligately? Not us. But it is everything we are. It falls freely from the sky. It carries us and our toys and joys. It is clouds and mist and fog and sleet and breath. There is no sweeter more crucial food. It ought to remind us of Your generosity every time we sip or swim or shower. It reminded me of You this morning. I bow gently in gratitude. And now, forgive me, I must be going, as there is a small boy hammering on the door and wailing and gnashing his teeth, and there is a disgruntled line forming behind him. And so: amen.

Prayer in Celebration of Brief Things, for Example, Church Services

Mayflies. Toddlers. Tree swallows. Apologies—isn't it interesting that the best and most genuine ones are short and to the point? The longer they go on the less honest they are, and the more they turn into insincere performances; see any politician's press conference ostensibly apologizing for his misbehavior, with his poor grim simmering spouse alongside for the photo op. But the brief admission of idiocy—that's delicious. *My bad* spoken clearly on the basketball court. The Mass that cuts to the chase and doesn't sprawl into performance art and endless self-absorbed homily. The quick wit, the bushtit, the postcard. The shorter saints like Teresa of Avila. The brief ride in the car and the short plane flight. The chapbook, the brief line at the bank, the hilarious thirty-second film clip. Young people only as tall as your knee, who generally see the world with fresher eyes and an admirable lack of agenda. Small cups of strong coffee. Small boys with short hair whose heads in the right light look exactly like peaches. Brief phone calls and electronic-mail missives that get to the point without undue blather and verbal fencing. Small sharp astonishing poems. Novellas. Pencil stubs. Tree frogs. Sandals. Brief heartfelt prayers. Like this one. And so: amen.

Desperate Prayer for Patience with Politicians with Excellent Suits and Shoes and Meticulous Hair and Gobs of Television Makeup Who Have Utterly Forgotten That Their Jobs Are Finally About Feeding and Clothing and Protecting and Schooling Children

They are driving me stark muttering bubbling insane. They are nattering and preening. They are dissembling and speechifying. They are evading the question and mouthing empty slogans. They are attacking straw men of their own devising and calculating market share. Their words are wind and dust and meanwhile children starve and are raped and have no beds and teachers and doctors. They say they will do things and they do not do those things. They appeal to the worst in us so as to be able to make money. They send children to war though they have never been in war and do not know the savagery of what they are sending children to do. They abuse their power and sneer at the poor and condescend to the elderly and lie about their motivations and their biographies. They would happily soil every lake and river and pond and creek and rivulet with every imaginable searing death-dealing chemical if there was enough money in it for them. They would foul every square meter of air with choking smoke and ash if there was enough money in it for them. They do not care about our children and our children's children. They pose for photo opportunities on the way to church but they do not feed the hungry and clothe the naked and house the homeless and slake the thirst of those who are desperate. Dear sweet Lord, give me the patience to be reasonable and call them calmly to account. Give them the startle of guilt and the ripple of shame. Make sore their consciences and shiver their arrogance so that they may puncture it themselves and so begin to achieve humility and be of actual honest genuine service to the least among us. This we pray, trying not to snarl overmuch. And so: amen.

Prayer for the Little Brown Birds Nesting in the Lavender Bushes by the Walnut Tree

Sparrows, I think, or maybe wrens. Or maybe wrens on steroids. I'd like to know just *where* they got those steroids, because *someone* is really going to regret selling growth hormone to birds in *my* yard . . . Oh, never mind, they're sparrows; I see the plumage better from this angle. Sorry about that. But how extraordinary they are, how liquid-quick, how alert and eager and sharp-eyed for seeds and nuts, how quick to slide away into the lavender when man or dog or squirrel approaches. Such dots of dash, such infinitesimal beings, not one of them as big as my fist. What a world, to have sparrows in it! And silently suddenly I ask You for their safety, the little comedians; keep them from the neighborhood cats, the coyotes in the ravine, the occasional gopher snake, the stooping kestrel; give them their daily bread, and their mysterious love affairs, and a peace that surpasseth understanding; grant them not one but two clutches of eggs, a plethora of nestlings to love and harbor—as You have granted me the same—and here they come now, sleepy and disheveled, wondering what I am watching so carefully by the walnut tree; and we stand together for a delicious moment; for which I thank You also. And so: amen.

Furious Prayer for the Church I Love and Have Always Loved but Which Drives Me Insane with Its Fussy Fidgety Prim Tin-Eared Thirst for Control and Rules and Power and Money Rather Than the One Simple Thing the Founder Insisted On

Granted, it's a tough assignment, the original assignment. I get that. Love—Lord help us, could we not have been assigned something easier, like astrophysics or quantum mechanics? But no—love those you cannot love. Love those who are poor and broken and fouled and dirty and sick with sores. Love those who wish to strike you on both cheeks. Love the blowhard, the pompous ass, the arrogant liar. Find the Christ in each heart, even those. Preach the Gospel and only if necessary talk about it. Be the Word. It is easy to advise and pronounce and counsel and suggest and lecture; it is not so easy to do what must be done without sometimes shrieking. Bring love like a bright weapon against the dark. The Rabbi did not say build churches, or retreat houses, or secure a fleet of cars for general use, or convene conferences, or issue position papers. He was pretty blunt about the hungry and the naked and the sick. He was not reasonable; we forget this. The Church is not a reasonable idea. The Church should be a verb. When it is only a noun it is not what the Founder asked of us. Let us pray that we are ever after dissolving the formal officious arrogant thing that wants to rise, and ever fomenting the contradictory revolutionary counter-cultural thing that could change life on this planet. It could, you know. Let's try again today. And so: amen.

Muttered Prayer in Thanks for the Under-Genius of Christmas

Putting up ye old fir tree last night, and pondering why again we slay a perfectly healthy tree ten years of age, not even a teenager yet, and prop up the body, and drape it with frippery, and then finally feed the brittle former vibrancy into a chipper, paying a grim Boy Scout five bucks for the privilege; I watched mine bride and children quietly for a while, from behind the tree where I was struggling with that haunted cursed string of lights, and I saw the under-genius of it all; I saw beneath the tinsel and nog, the snarl of commerce and the ocean of misspent money; I saw the quiet pleasure of ritual, the actual no-kidding no-fooling urge to pause and think about other people and their joy, the anticipation of days spent laughing and shouldering in the kitchen, with no agenda and no press of duty. I saw the flash of peace and love under all the shrill selling and tinny theater; and I was thrilled and moved. And then I remembered too that the ostensible reason for it all was the Love being bold and brave enough to assume a form that would bleed and break and despair and die; and I was again moved, and abashed; and I finished untangling the epic knot of lights, shivering yet again with happiness that we were given such a sweet terrible knot of a world to untangle, as best we can, with bumbling love. And so: amen.

Prayer of Thanks for All Birds, Herons in Particular

For their *heronness*, you know what I mean? The way they are long, and thin, and still, and elegant, and shaggy, and awkward, and not at all awkward, and lean, and gangly, and knobby-kneed, and bluegray-brown all at once, and slow and dinosauric in the air but liquid-quick with their bladed beaks. I never yet saw a heron that did not instantly amaze and astound and confound and provoke something very much like awe. Is the divine spark in the heron? Yes. In its ferocious murder of the frog, and startling-quick gobbling of the frog, leaving only one webbed foot wriggling for a last moment in the world it just left? Yes, somehow. In the big red-ruddered hawk who descends upon the heron like a burly nightmare and tears its breast from its spindly bones? Yes, somehow. In all of this is the Breath, the Imagination, the voice that said *I am who am* from a fiery bush, long ago. In the beauty of the animals who grew to be herons and hawks over millions of years of experimentation. In the wiry wave of reeds in which this story was written before my eyes one day on a river headed to the sea. In the mink and the crows who will also eat the rest of the heron. In the musing man standing hidden in the alder thicket; he too is here fishing for mysterious life for a moment until a dark hawk comes for him; but meanwhile he knows enough to sing his companions in the wild miracle of the worlds we share. And so: amen.

Prayer for Hospital Chaplains

Of any creed and religion and tradition and spiritual practice whatsoever, for they are the ones who knock gently on the doors of patients who are dazed and afraid and in pain, and stick their heads in and ask gently if they can be of service, and many times endure the lash of rude and vulgar response, and have to accept that as the price of doing business; and they are the ones who sometimes walk softly into the room and lay hands on hands or heads and whisper prayers and ask for blessings and healing and restored strength if at all possible, and those are hard things to ask for when the being in the bed is so patiently broken and bruised and frightened and helpless no matter how hard you pray or how huge your empathetic heart; and they are the ones who then knock on the next door and the next, day after day week after week, sometimes for many years like a dear friend of mine who became a priest after a while just so he could bring the sacraments to those bedsides. They are a great sweet patient diligent amazing tribe, chaplains; and this morning, in the chapel of the hospital with its huge windows and small simple unadorned crucifix, I pray for them, with all my heart. And so: amen.

Prayer for My Brother

My brother was a mathematician. My late brother. He died at age sixty-four. He would be sixty-six today. Numbers, numbers. He weighed 250 at his apex and 150 when he died. Where did those one hundred pounds go? Eaten by his cancer. A hungry disease, starving for a mathematician. Now he weighs one pound in his stone box in the soil under an oak tree. For years he was a numbers theorist, contemplating the mysteries of his beloved discipline. It is a language, he told me. It is a sort of music. We use numbers to say things. When it all snicks into place in a proof or a theorem it is something like love, he said. He had two children and one wife and six brothers and one sister. We use numbers to say things. He was seventy-five inches tall. He used few words. I thought he was stern but discovered he was shy. Maybe numbers were his way of writing poems and essays and letters. He thought that the Breath was a mathematician. The genius of genius mathematicians, he said. All mathematics leads back that way. Or forward too. Time is mathematics. The spin of the earth, the sprawl of stars, the leap of light. All mathematics. And so: amen.

Prayer of Thanks for Old Girlfriends, or Boyfriends, as the Case May Be

No, we don't think about them much if at all anymore, and yes, it all worked out right that we are not together, and no, it would not have been a good idea at all to continue on in what became a murky emotional wilderness, but yes, we should be grateful that they came into our lives, or that we blundered into theirs; for in many ways they are how we came to be who we are, isn't that so? And didn't we learn how to love better by loving generally poorly and awkwardly in the opening chapters, before moving up to the current big leagues? Isn't that so? We muddled, we prevaricated, we took them for granted, we were not as gentlemanly as we could have been; we stayed too long with them when we knew in our hearts that we did not love them deeply enough to take the leap of faith; we happily blamed them when we broke up when really deep in our hearts we knew whose fault it was. So thank You for the pain and confusion and thrill of first and second and third loves; thank You for letting us muddle along learning to be painfully honest and not try to be cool and not hold on desperately to that which is rightfully leaving the scene; thank You for the bruise of education, and the joy of the much deeper confusion of marriage. Deft work there, Friend. And so: amen.

Prayer of Spitting Inchoate Rage That You Allow Such Things & People to Inflict Such Horrendous Pain & Agony, Especially on Little Kids, How Could You Let That *Happen*?

Even though I suspect You are as enraged as I am. Even as I suspect You are not in the business of interfering with what we are stammering toward ever so slowly as a species. Even though I suspect You breathed everything into being, dreamed it, and then spoke it like an explosion in the unimaginable Not, and then let it roll, hoping You were right and we would rise to our genius, which is You. Even though I snarl at people who attack You for not stopping slime like Cardinal Bernard Law and Osama bin Laden and Mao Zedong, that they are not Your business, Your business is creation, not policing thugs, as far as I can tell. Even though I have dark splinters of things like rage and greed in my own heart. Even so. So I come to You abashed and praying for something I cannot articulate—some tidal wave of mercy, some flash of shame in such men, in all of us who do ill when we know full well in each chamber of our hearts that someone suffers for what we gain.

How can You have allowed us to make such a world, where children are raped every blessed day, where a species dies forever every blessed day, where millions watch television as millions more starve? How could You have given us such freedom? But You did, You did; and so my prayer must be finally for me, to work harder against the dark, to sing louder, to find more teammates, is that right? Your silence is eloquent again; as usual; as always. And so: amen.

Prayer in Thanks for (Small) Pains

Because we do need them, of course. Not the big savage awful ones; those we can do without, and no, suffering teaches us nothing, and is not a gift to bring us close to He who suffered unto death. That's silly talk. But the small pains, the sore ankle, the pulled muscle, the common cold, the cut over the eye that needs three stitches, the jammed finger, the stiff knee—those are humbling, those are real, those are honest, they remind us that our vehicles have warranty periods, they remind us that we are not golden gods, they reduce arrogance and make us alive and alert again to the fact that people bend over backward for us all day long. We have all been sick and huddled in bed moaning piteously and had someone putter in here and there with hot water and another blanket and two crackers and that book you always wanted to read when you had three days of uninterrupted time, which you now have, and how *did* this glorious soul remember that?

For the sore shoulder, thanks; for the back spasm that goes away after a while, thanks; for the sneezing fit and scratchy throat, again God bless me I just had this a month ago, thanks; for the mild flu that wipes out your kid and gives you the chance to sit at the edge of his bed and stroke his hair and want to weep with amazement that he came into your life somehow despite the fact that you are no way going to be a great dad because you are just a mule but by gawd you will try to be the best dad ever, thanks; for the small pains that remind us sharply of so many companions on the road who suffer savagely right this instant and deserve every scrap and shred of prayer, thanks; and in closing hold them in the palm of Your hand and breathe hope into them? And also maybe just for fun quash this back spasm thing that started Wednesday? And so: amen.

Prayer of Bemused Thanks for Scrunchies & Those Other Weird Lovely Things Women Wear in Their Hair

Which is, of course, a prayer of thanks for women, every one of them beautiful beyond words, not that I am looking closely or anything. But they *are*. Brilliant and silly and generous and graceful and sinewy and amused by clunky burly male animals. And o gawd their hair spilling and cascading and rippling and sliding over their shoulders, their hair cupping those extraordinary faces! I have never once seen a woman who was not beautiful; even those who were churlish and surly, those who most obviously and assiduously used their beauty as tool and weapon, those who drew plaudits in business for being as cold and greedy as male captains of industry were girls still somewhere inside, and liable to flashes of tenderness and grace. I was granted one above all, to witness and to celebrate, to sing and to explore, though there will never be an end to her mystery, never; and I was granted a daughter, to witness and to protect, and finally to launch into the world, far away; and I was granted a vision of all those scrunchies and clasps, clicking and snapping hair-pieces, buried headlong in the wildernesses of their voluminous hair; and it is another mysterious gift of Yours, I know, that the women I have met who have lost their hair, and beam at me bald as doorknobs despite the wither of their illness, are more beautiful than they were before; how could that be? Yet it is so. For their fullness and their litheness, for their patience and their testiness, for their endless complexity and their oceanic empathy, thank You. And this is not even to get into the whole kissing thing, *another* great idea. And so: amen.

Prayer on Seeing Yet Another Egregious Parade of Muddy Paw Prints on the Floor

Remember, my friends, that someday there will come a day when this holy being will not be capable of leaving muddy paw prints, and that will be a hard cold day, for he was a companion of endless eager cheer and amiability, who never nipped or bit any of us, and who daily greeted us at the back door with an open-hearted welcome that many times elevated a weary heart; and though yes, he did wreak havoc among the squirrels and moles, and capture and eat many of them, still, that was the evolutionary path assigned to him by the Dreamer, and the moles ate many a worm without anyone shrieking in dismay about that. Remember that he taught us much about the world on our walks with him, in his ferocious attentiveness to all things, especially their scents; and remember too that he was a playful being, and knew full well the joy of games and horseplay, and relished every moment of that, and hardly drooled at all, and was thorough about cleaning up spilled tidbits with a startling alacrity in a being so physically commanding; you never saw a dog the size of a pony leap after a lost meatball with such blinding speed, and that is not a sight granted unto us all that much by the Filmmaker. Remember that the dog was sweet and gentle and friendly and funny, and ever he was kindhearted and generous with his time and affection, and there is much to admire in that, so let us just get a ragged old towel from the mud room, and clean up the paw prints before the boss of the house gets home, and that will be a sort of prayer also, an act of diligent attentiveness while on your knees. And so: amen.

Prayer in Reluctant but Abashed Hesitant Appreciation of Death

Oddly it's not *my* eventual death that frightens and nags me; *I* have had a glorious blessed hilarious graced life, and no man was ever so slathered with love and laughter as me, and when my time to dissolve comes, I hope to acquiesce with some modicum of grace, and remember that I was granted a long and colorful run; indeed I hope to spend eons happily reviewing the tape, minute by minute, paying even more attention to the infinitesimal details than I did the first time, and replaying the highlights again and again, driving my new roommates nuts. No: it's the death of people I love that ravages me. My brother Seamus, who was about to walk for the first time. My brother Christopher, born and baptized and dead the same day. My brother Kevin, tottering from cancer but grinning and making wry brilliant remarks to the very end. (*The answer is in the questioning,* his last six words—ponder *that* for a year.) My dear friend Bob Boehmer, the most gentlemanly man I ever met, and him a soldier of the Great War, and a football star, and a boxer. The child my lovely bride and I lost twenty years ago, when he or she was the size of a thumb, a child I very much wish to meet, someday. My sweet gentle cousin Maureen the nun. So many friends. So many children of friends. So many young soldiers and brave terrified holy children. I get the idea, Lord; I understand we come and we go; I understand that it is a vast recycling project; and that all things must pass, and that somehow this is a mysterious part of the genius of Your gift; I get it. But it stabs us to the quick, and I lie awake in the deep reaches of the night fearing pain and death reaching for my sweet wild children; yet I know I must thank You for the dark door, somehow, for reasons beyond my ken; but do not think me ungrateful when I whisper those thanks and do not shout them, for I am sore afraid, and saddened too deeply for words; and I can only trust that those I love will be waiting for me with open arms and the entertaining tape of my life; and my friends and brothers will have already flagged the egregious idiot moments for high hilarity; and there will be good beer; and all manner of things will be well. And so: amen.

Prayer of Thanks for Stephen John Nash, of What Is Today Called British Columbia

Because he was for a long while not the best basketball player in the world but the most creative and imaginative and visionary and generous. Because he was the most valuable player in the best basketball league in the world not once but twice and he was one of the smallest slightest unmuscularest players ever. Because he got better with age without major drugs, and how often can you say that of someone who sells his quickness and vision for cash? Because for a while he was arguably the best point guard in the world, and truly point guards are close to God, having some of the same profligate urge to share. Because he reportedly ate absolutely no sugar for ten years, which is stunning and monastic. Because he is the best Catholic point guard since John Stockton. Because unlike many of the other men who work in his profession, he has a sense of humor and an eloquent rage against injustice and lies. Because he never was arrested in the company of women named Krystl and Sparkl. Because he is the father of twins, and so has had many a sleepless night, with small people barfing on his shoulders. Because people leant forward in their seats or on their couches or bar stools when he got the ball and the fast break began, because they might see something they had never seen before, which is exactly why we love basketball, and exactly the feeling you have when you have those little rippling epiphanies here and there about the nature of creation in the largest arena, as it were, which is not in Phoenix, but *is* rife with Suns. Because while it may seem that basketball is a game, it is more like a creative art in some hands, and his hands were some of those hands in recent years, for which I thank You, Coach. Nice job. Deft and admirable work there. And so: amen.

Prayer for the Men & Women Who Huddle Inside Vast Rain Slickers All Day Holding Up STOP Signs at Construction Sites & Never Appear to Shriek in Despair & Exhaustion

---

I pray for warmth for you. Less rain. No idiot drivers whizzing past and splashing your pants and boots. I pray that there is quiet sweet music in your head. I pray that you are getting paid decent wages and that you do not have a head cold or pneumonia. I pray in appreciation for what seems like an oceanic patience and endurance on your part. I pray a little in abashed appreciation of the fact that I am in a warm car on the way to work and not standing in the pelting sideways icy rain wrapped in eight layers of clothes with a walkie-talkie in one hand and a STOP sign in the other and idiot drivers whizzing past despite the many signs that say please slow down people are working hard here in the rain. I pray that you are a sort of mystic who considers an eight-hour shift at your post a heck of a good day when the sun comes out for five minutes and you see an osprey with a trout. I pray that a good part of your day is affectionate razzing and teasing and laughing with your coworkers. I pray that none of you gets hurt by the huge pipes and slabs of concrete and tremendous cranes wheeling and roaring overhead. I pray in gratitude for the way the bridge you are building is really in the end a conduit for people to work on behalf of their children's health and joy. I pray that someone pulls over, here and there, and gets out of his car, and brings you hot coffee or cookies or even maybe three lilies, just because, because no particular reason other than he too has seen you there day after day smiling as we wave and he too thinks you are one cool holy being and someone should once in a while get out of his car and say so. And so: amen.

Prayer for Osama bin Laden Yes Even Him the Stupid Murderous Slime

Because if I cannot pray grudgingly ragingly reluctantly furiously confusedly complicatedly for *his* shattered soul, what is the point of praying at all? Yes, even him, the man who murdered thousands of innocents, among them Christine Hanson, age three, and Dana Falkenberg, age three, and David Brandhorst, age three, and Julia McCourt, age four. Among them Dana's sister Zoe, who I am absolutely sure was huddling her little sister in her arms as the plane exploded. Even him, the man who cackled in his cave when he heard of the success of his plans. Who cackled at the roasting of small children. But there must have been a shard of holiness in that man, at least originally; there must have been a small shriveled soul once; maybe there was some small shivering moment much later, as he sat wrapped in his robes in Abbottabad watching himself on an endless video loop, the narcissistic ass, when he felt a flicker of shame at what he had done, at how he had wasted his life, at how he had endangered the very faith he so adamantly insisted he was defending. I hope so. I pray. I pray that somehow somewhere sometime he wept at his copious sins. I pray that his dark energy was dissolved by the Mercy and cleaned by love and sent to redeem itself as the engines of insects and birds and tiny fish in clear pools. I pray that I am right and there is a Forgiveness bigger than any slime and that somehow in ways I do understand but believe in with awe and not a little fear that You have found a chamber in Your heart for even him. Even him. And so: amen.

Prayer for All the Dads of the Girls I Dated Before Winning the Girl Lottery *Big Time*

Sirs, I apologize. I saw your suspicious glances and I airily issued promises to you, but then, yes, I did maul your daughters gently, and gaze at them with relentlessly amorous intent, and never did actually entertain the slightest honorable intention as regards marriage and full and fervid support of their dreams and ambitions. Sirs, I am sorry. I can plead only youth and its inherent narcissism. I can atone now only by this public apology and by doing my utmost, as the husband of a vision, to witness her grace and hard work, and do whatever I can to be of assistance to her dreams and ambitions, so that in some odd way she stands for all women, and thus in some small way I expiate my behavior when I was dating your admirable daughters. Also while I am in the confessional booth here I apologize specifically to the one among you who probably still to this day has the trunk key of a 1969 Impala in his lawn, where it has resided for many years, and probably occasionally caused the lawnmower to gasp and choke. My bad. I threw the keys in the air that night in roaring frustration over the status of my muddled relationship at that time with your admirable daughter, and while I did, after searching for more than an hour on my hands and knees in your meticulous lawn, recover the ignition key, I did not, as you probably know, find the trunk key, which caused some problems with the owner of the car, my own dad, but which also perhaps caused your lawnmower indigestion over the years, for which, once again, my most sincere apologies. In closing, my best wishes and regards, and allow me to entertain you somewhat with the startling news that I too, sirs, now have a teenage daughter, and soon enough will be placed in your former position, from which, sirs, I expect to enjoy the chance to terrify some poor young idiot, and glare at him with patent distrust, and examine my lawn carefully occasionally, just in case. And so: amen.

Prayer of Thanks for Hoes & Scythes & Spatulas & Toothbrushes & Binoculars & the Myriad Other Tools & Instruments That Fit Our Hands So Gracefully & Allow Us to Work with a Semblance of Deftitude

Lovely little inventions, just right for the job at hand—a lawn edger, for example, or an arrow, or the keyboard on which I hammer this sentence. Thank You for giving our species the chance to be creative. Thank You for giving us the chance to bring ideas to bear against illness. Thank You for giving us a chance to keep evolving past violence and greed and toward a real communion of souls no matter what color or language or religion or personal angle on the world. Thank You for giving us a chance to rise from mold to our current astonishing wet machinery. Thank You for letting everything else rise too in all sorts of wild directions. Thank You for starting the ball rolling whenever and however it was exactly You did that, which we of course are not quite sure of at the moment. Thank You for letting us rise to be mostly curious and energetic beings itching to find out why and how and if. Thank You for not being a

Dictator. Thank You for the mystery of why You are letting loose to make a better world or ruin it. You puzzle us; we beseech You constantly for intercession; but we know full well in our deepest hearts that some aspect of Your genius is to let us try for the light on our own. We hate that, sometimes; but we pray in gratitude for Your mysterious Wisdom. And so: amen.

Prayer to the Madonna

Yes, sometimes it feels a little odd to be addressing my
most heartfelt and searing and thankful and terrified
prayers to a woman who was a shy calm Jewish girl of
maybe fifteen when a shock of light appeared in your
house (kitchen? back bedroom? we've never been clear
on that.), and everything changed forever for everyone,
but I *know* you are for real, and I *know* you can hear me,
and I know this in the core of my soul and bones, and I
don't understand how, and I don't care to understand,
and there's no way to ever prove or explain what I
know, but *you* know, which is why here I am again, this
morning, mumbling in your general direction, which
is everywhere. Your mercy, your capacious tenderness,
your open ear, the soothe of your voice in me and out
there at the same time; I can never explain to anyone
how I hear you and feel your gentle hand, but I do, and
many times it has sustained and saved me in times of
great sadness and fear; so it is that I sit here this morning and am grateful. Thank you for being beyond my
sense and apprehension. Thank you for saying yes not
once thousands of years ago but all day every day in
ways far beyond my ken. Thank you for being beyond
a name and a body now but alive and vibrant in every

moment. Thank you for saving me when I stood at the abyss. Thank you for holding my children in the star-furnace of your love. Thank you for catching my spirit when I crumple and dissolve and my body fades and everything I was is gathered and slathered and shaped anew. Thank you for this moment. Thank you for being in it with me. And so: amen.

Prayer for the Girl Scouts of America

Those small brave cheerful chirping green children, selling me sugar in incredible doses every year, trapping people grimly as they try to enter the library and the grocery store. You have to admire the devious system; who could say no to a person no taller than your waist, accompanied by her grinning tiny compatriots, all in uniform, with a beaming maternal bookkeeper behind the table? Not me. And for all I know I will probably have to cut another notch in my belt with the tip of the steak knife when no one is looking, and for all I know surely some percentage of my contribution will buy whiskey and dancing shoes for the Scout leadership in New York City, still, it seems cool to me that there are two million Girls Scouts in America, and nearly another million American moms helping them out, and some ten million Girl Scouts and Girl Guides in 145 countries around this particular planet, and all of this effort in the end is about joy and teamwork and friendship and laughter and travel and waking up to things and people you didn't know and might never have discovered on your own, and these all seem like excellent things. So as I wangle the box of Thin Mints open and have just one and then pop another as a sort of comparative research project, I think of all those grinning girls with their braces and pigtails and barrettes and sneakers and voices like sparrows and I actually no kidding pray for them—for their joy, their safety, their wild sweet small holiness. It is a better world for those small green people in it, and that is a fact. And so: amen.

Prayer on Good Friday

Which isn't good at all. One of the great misnomers of all time. It's bleak, haunted, immensely sad. It rivets and ravages me every year as I sit hidden behind a post-beam in the balcony of the chapel, where no one can see me weeping at the poor lonely broken Yeshua, betrayed by His best friends, beaten by the sneering cops, blood dripping into His eyes, grilled by a police chief who couldn't care less about justice and mercy and wants only to evade blame for a matter he considers minor at best. Yet it wasn't minor at all, and somehow it turns on that harrowing day long ago. A mysterious young man from a country village, causing an epic political and civil ruckus in the city. A murderous mob, angry religious Brahmins, potential colonial unrest that will *not* look good at headquarters. Gnomic answers by the calm young man when interrogated. Poor Peter bitterly berating himself for his cowardice, and which one of us would have done better? The apostles frightened, the sound of hammers nailing the young man to a cross, the lowering darkness, the murmurs of fear through the city as the sun is blotted out. Veronica's veil and Simon's shoulders, Simon the African; did his compassion surge and make him step forth, or was he shoved into legend by a soldier? The gaunt young man sagging toward death; His quiet blessing of a thief; His last words to His mother; one last desperate cry; He thirsts, He prays, He dies. And in the chapel not another word, not another sound; and soon we exit silently, and go our ways, for once without the tang of Eucharist on our tongues, for once without a cheerful chaff for friends and handshakes all round; and no matter how bright the rest of the day, how brilliant the late afternoon, how redolent the new flowers, how wild the sunset over the river, you shiver a little; not just for Him, but for all of us, His children, face to face today with despair. And so silently home to pray for light emerging miraculously where it seemed all was dark. And so: amen.

Prayer for Opossums, You Poor Ugly Disdained Perfect Creatures

Ah, we say they are ugly, and they look like insane cats on major psychotropic drugs, but (a) other possums don't think they are ugly, and (b) the Lord of All Things set them in motion, so, you know, who are we to get snotty about appearance? Also can you imagine what they think of *our* appearance, our ludicrously brief tails and teeth as dense as fences? Maybe all beings are beautiful and we would be wise to admit this. Maybe all things that live are beautiful beyond understanding, even the New York Yankees. Maybe life is the very definition of beauty and all this attention on the exterior is shallow and stupid. I mean, look in your own life: Aren't the most beautiful souls you know hardly ever the most handsome or pretty ones? Isn't exterior beauty sort of dangerous for the person inside, who so easily can get sucked into believing it matters, or even worse learning how to use it for money and power? Aren't all women beautiful and all men handsome in their hilarious unhandsomeness? So let us join tails and teeth in celebration of the possum, the poster child for the beauty of what is; and ask the Designer to lend us wisdom in the matter of seeing miracles clearly all around us; including, unbelievably but truly, in the two incredible creatures hissing and snarling nasally on the fence above the garbage can. And so: amen.

Prayer for Women Named Ethel and Men Named Elmer, for We Will Not See Their Likes Again

Also Edna and Edith and Eustace, and cool hoary names like that that reek of American character and dignity and hard work and lace doilies on Sunday before the roast. For all the brave tough quiet generous unassuming souls who came before us and built this country and built our cities and farmed the generous land and raised their children and never asked for much except a chance to breathe free and love widely. For all those who bore names that we would grin at today but they didn't think were funny. For their rough worn hands and their seamed leathery faces that endured a lot of weather and war and pain and loss but they kept working and loving anyway. For those who came to this country with names in other languages and forged new lives but never lost their love for the lands they left behind. For those who bear the names of their brave wild sweet ancestors with pride. For those who name their children for extraordinary souls in the fervent hope something of the sanctity and courage of the named will shower their beloved new babies. For names, which are mere sounds and handles, but which mean so much to so many. And so: amen.

Prayer for the Reader Who Photocopies This Prayer and Shares It with Friends and Sisters

Dear Coherence: Thank You for beer and friends and pencils and socks and the Red Cross and cellos and Paul Desmond's saxophone and Wiffle balls and elm trees and woodpeckers and transistor radios in the pockets of old men who are fishing for bass and perch but also keeping one ear on the baseball game. Thank You for suspenders and Larry Bird. Thank You for typewriter keys and stamps and windowpanes and coffeepots. Thank You for Rosemary Clooney's voice especially in her later years. Thank You for photocopy machines and friends and sisters and the refrigerators on which we pin up small lovely strange things people we love send us in the mail. Thank You for teeth and earphones. Thank You for sand crabs and seat belts. Thank You for the way that men pat their pockets while checking for their keys and wallets and phones. Thank You for the way people defer to each other while boarding the bus. Thank You for all the little things that are not little. Absolutely beautiful work there. If You had a supervisor I would *so* be writing a letter of commendation for Your personnel file, but . . . And so: amen.

Prayer in Gratitude for the Right Song Arriving at the Right Time, for Example Samuel Barber's *Adagio for Strings* or Bruce Springsteen's "The Rising," or Chet Baker's "She Was Too Good to Me"

Because you know and I know that a song can save your life. We know that and we don't say it much, but it's true. When you are dark and despairing a song comes and makes you weep as you think *yes yes yes*. When you are joyous a song comes to top off the moment and make you think the top of your head will fly off from sheer fizzing happy. A song makes you sob with sadness for such pain and loss as throbs inside the bars of the song. A song roars that we will not be defeated by murder but we will stand together and rise again, brothers and sisters! A song makes your heart stagger that you found someone to love with such an ache and a pang. A song comes—how amazing and sweet and glorious that is. And this is not even to get into how amazing and miraculous music itself is, the greatest of all arts. But this evening, haunted by a song that slid out of the radio and lit up your heart, we pray in thanks that there are such fraught wild holy moments as this one. And so: amen.

Prayer of Bemused Appreciation for Handheld Mobile Devices

Which seemed like the utensils of the devil when we first apprehended them in the greedy paws of our children and other young delinquents, but it turns out they are useful and entertaining little machines, by which you can keep track of your children and their misdemeanors, and debate your lovely bride about who ought to get coffee and milk on the way home, and make your friends laugh with brief rude haikus, and receive sudden stunning photographs from friends and family, and catch little sweet moments that heretofore would have been inarguably harder to catch. Yes, they are addictive for some people, and yes, they shatter and dissolve attention spans among their younger users, and yes, some people I could name need to learn that not every stray thought they have ought to be promulgated, and yes, tweeting is silly and self-absorbed most of the time, but still . . . They are creative inventions, and they do make life a little safer when the old battalion tank of a car breaks down and you need roadside assistance, and most of all they are a way to stay abreast and connected and engaged with your kids, which is really crucial, isn't it? So, Designer, thank you . . . I guess. And so: amen.

Prayer for Sunday Morning

Well, first that another one came around; thank You for letting me breathe another day. And thanks for the scrap of sunlight, finally, after seventy no kidding *seventy* straight days of rain and mist and adamant cloud cover, but who's complaining? And thanks for the shaggy lazy peace of Sunday morning, and the obese newspaper, and the way you can stay in your bathrobe, and the way bacon is allowed, and the way people shuffle into the kitchen yawning and happy, and the way there's no agenda except a vague shower schedule so as to make Mass. And thanks for Sunday Mass, which can be pro forma and dull and formal and check-the-box, but most of the time isn't; most of the time it's warm and funny and populous and communal, and sometimes it's even moving, and there are always babies and usually dogs, and you can sit in the back under the glowing windows and remember that the Catholic Church isn't a huge corporation as much as it is a vast amalgam of small villages in which people hold hands against the dark and believe in the unbelievable. Isn't that wild and cool? Well—You knew that. But I am just saying thanks, this morning, after coffee, and before I get the last shower, which is reserved for Dad, because he can stand the cold water best, I guess. And so: amen.

Prayer in Thanks for the Little Flying Dinosaurs We Call Dragonflies

Because they are unbelievably cool, that's why, and we casually glance at them when they whiz past, and rarely if ever sit down in a daze and contemplate the fact that they are astonishing miracles, the saber-toothed tigers of the insect world, and they are the most amazing aeronautical engineers and fighter pilots, and they come in all colors, and sometimes on a hot day there are dozens of them in the air all at once, stitching patterns and conducting maneuvers that I would have given a thousand bucks for in the old days when I was a young supple athlete; to move like that, changing directions in a split second, wow! But then my mind suddenly is filled with dragonflies in basketball shorts and soccer jerseys, so we had better close up shop with this prayer, and yet again, for what must be the millionth time in fifty years, thank the Engineer for absolutely first-rate design and construction. What an artist, what craft, what imaginative leaps! And so: amen.

Prayer in Gratitude for Sisters Related to You by Blood

Even if, you know, they punched you out here and there when you were little, which the fact is you deserved a sharp jab here and there; but other than the occasional bruise, which you deserved, your sisters were generally sweet and funny and always there when you needed help and always wry and piercing with advice whether you asked for it or not. And they quietly became dear friends, really, didn't they? And while when you were young it was weird to think that a person with your genetic fingerprints could be so completely female, somehow in subtle fashion that became educational and enlightening and elevating, didn't it? And now when you think of your sisters don't you smile right away and take a long time to remember that sharp jab? So a prayer for sisters, holy beings all, despite all their incredible misadventures; for they were gifts from the Breath, and they remain mysterious gentle gifts, and they bless us. And so: amen.

Prayer for Sisters Not Related to You by Blood

And there are so *many*, isn't that amazing and lovely and refreshing and something you lean on here and there, quietly delighted? Don't we all have about eight more sisters in life than the ones who were also in mom's womb on other lease arrangements? Friends of our lovely brides, sisters-in-law, fellow conspirators in our occupations and avocations, the wives of brothers, the wives of brothers-in-law, the teachers of our children . . . they are everywhere, these sudden sisters, and You are a deft and profligate and subtle Grace to give us female friends who are *friends* and not prospective kissing partners, women of whom you can safely and happily say *boy I dig that odd sweet soul* and not get the laser death stare from your lovely bride. Thank You for them, for their humor and generosity, for the way they add zest and verve and. . . . And so: amen.

Prayer of Thanks for Suntan Lotion

Which smells good; which smells like relaxed; which smells like little giggling children in peculiar and hilarious bathing suits; which smells like not-working; which evokes summer; which smacks of the beach and sand and gulls and terns and salt air and beer; which comes in bright colorful containers; which sometimes needs to be lovingly ladled on the backs of lovely spouses and children, a moment that always gives me the happy willies; which never actually expires but can be used eleven years later after you find a nearly dry container in the very back of the medicine cabinet; which finally just by the faint scent of it reminds me most powerfully and movingly of my children; so thank You, Light. And so: amen.

Prayer of Thanks for the Game of Chess

Bless me, *what* a great invention, if you evade the whole clashing-armies motif for a moment. What a game of wit and patience! What a game of riveted attentiveness! Is there another game in the world that requires you to enter humbly into the mind of another person, and reside there for an hour, and assume that he or she is smarter than you are, and try to apprehend and anticipate his or her sly devious subtle creativity, in the manner that chess does? Let us pretend for a moment that indeed it was invented in Afghanistan or India by human beings, even as we know that You lit the spark that became our creativity. And let us express our humble gratitude for a game that distracts us from active violence, and promotes friendship and discourse across the many lines and walls and borders and assumptions that divide us, and can be played by small children and ancient codgers like yours truly, and is often passed down with great love and affection from one generation to another, from older siblings to the young, and is played in parks and schools and church basements and beaches and castles and prisons all over the world, and sharpens wits and calms the soul, and costs nothing to play except your genuine full-on attention, which the more we sharpen our attentiveness the closer we are to You and the more we see Your fingerprints on all things; for which we bow and thank You yet again, Grand Master. And so: amen.

Prayer for the Boys I Used to Coach When They Were Little Unlike Now

Now they are mostly all taller than me, and their voices are deep, and some of them have that mortifying first scraggle of earnest facial hair, and one of them has a bright red Mohawk haircut that doesn't actually look too bad, and every time one of them sees me at the grocery store or the library he says hey, and I say o my goodness you are eight feet taller than you were in fourth grade, and we chat a while, and I always shuffle away moved almost to tears. They were so young, so small, so eager, so goofy, so skinny, so awkward. Two of them were happier in the gym at practice and at games than they were in either of their parents' homes. Several of them discovered over the three years that I coached them that they loved the game and still play it. Even now, seven years later, they can accurately recite my mantras about how to play the game right; they do so sometimes in the store, laughing as passersby look at us like we are nuts. Please, Lord, I beg You, keep these boys in Your hand and heart; make glancing the blows they will be dealt by life; lead them to work of substance, to the lovers who will savor and cherish them, to lives of joy and peace; for I loved them, Lord, I did, even though I can't say that to anyone else but You who will know quite what I mean. I loved their wild sweet untrammeled energy and their open genuine artless trust in me; and I miss them, Lord, I miss them terribly. And now I am crying; but You know what I feel, don't You? You feel that way with us, don't You? And so: amen.

Prayer for Firemen & Firewomen & Fire Chiefs & Fire Crews

Bravest among us, with soldiers and cops and mothers; they are the tall young calm efficient effective soothing souls who show up at three in the morning when trouble comes; they are there when the house next door begins to burn; they protect and watch out for us, their neighbors their friends their fellow citizens; they must have moments of awful fear and ennui, but they forge on relentless against pain and loss and disaster; and so this morning, after the flooded basement last night, and the emergency call across the street last week, and the burning house around the corner last year, and the sound of your sirens before dawn on Sunday morning, sprinting to rescue more of us, I pray for your safety and health, for even more eerie calm and remarkable strength and discipline granted unto you; and when you are no longer tall and sinewy and able to be sleepless for sixty hours without a break, may you be granted peace and joy and love unending from those you love; and may you know somehow in your bones that you and your work were admired more than you will ever be able to measure; and that there are many of us who think of you when we hear the word *hero*. And so: amen.

Prayer of Thanks for Good Bishops, as Opposed to Meatheads Who Think They Are Important

Like the archbishop we had here for fifteen years, and fifteen glorious years they were too, for they began with him saying loud and bold in public for attribution, pronouncing the words slowly and clearly and inarguably *I am your servant* and *I am the boss of no one*. Refreshing start, that. And then he also said that the rapes of children during the time of his predecessors was a sin, and that he would do everything in his power to apologize to and address the financial concerns of the victims and their families, and he would make sure it never happened again, and he would not dodge or prevaricate or lie or avoid or obfuscate the matter, for example by claiming that the rapists were not employees of the diocese; and all this even when he had not been here and had nothing to do with the past. And he welcomed every race and color and gender and age of people into the big tent of the Church he was responsible for; and he welcomed back people who had faded away for one reason or another; and he learned to speak two other languages so he could speak to large numbers of his congregation in their native tongue; and when he retired, as he had to by Church law at age seventy-five, there was great mourning that he would no longer be our chieftain, even though he said he was the boss of no one. To have a boss who understands he is your servant in the Word; that is what I pray for this evening, for all of us in this Church, for all of us who walk the road of the Word Incarnate. And so: amen.

Prayer for Deceased Great Old Catholic Magazines like *The Critic* and *Jubilee* and *The Ave Maria*

Which were not only intelligent and challenging and often loaded with great art and photography, but felt good in your hands, and flopped open invitingly on your desk or kitchen table, and were deeply devoted to the Catholic idea but not especially respectful of stuffy authoritarianism in Our Beloved Mother the Church; and which welcomed and published fascinating writers like Thomas Merton and Barry Lopez and the grapho-maniac Father Andrew Greeley; and which were read by millions of people all told which is a lot of heads and hearts being jazzed by the idea that we can indeed with concerted action and spiritual intent make a better sweeter more peaceful more joyous more equitable world; and which are now closed and deceased, shut down and relegated to archives and shelves, long gone except in memory; but I sing them here and offer a prayer for their founders and editors and writers and photographers and artists and circulation managers and deliverymen and telephone receptionists and advertising salesfolk and printers and janitors and paper vendors, who collectively worked for a world where violence is a memory and cruelty is a word you have to look up in the dictionary. It was good work, and they did it well, and I ask politely that You keep all those inky souls in Your capacious editorial hand, in whatever lively newsroom they now occupy. And so: amen.

Prayer for Publishers of Catholic Magazines & Newspapers

That they remain eager and challenging and creative, and do not censor themselves or their authors, and remember that they are every bit as crucial in the delivery of the Word as anyone else in the Church Eternal; and that they do not ask for permission from ostensible authority, but fling wide their nets for searing stories of grace and forgiveness and mercy in action in this bruised lovely broken miraculous world; and that they devote ever more of their epic talents to figuring out ways to appeal to and draw young people to the table to discuss the bones and sinews of Catholicism, which is the roaring search for humility and witness and kindness and generosity in a world that mostly seems to reward violence and greed and narcissism; and that they keep biting and kicking for ways to keep the budget going so they can indeed catch and share stories that *matter* so much more than the celebrity natter and scandal babble that crowds our media with its shrill tinny empty flash and gleam; and that they do not lose heart, but remember that they too are apostles and disciples on the road, carrying a message of crucial import, and that every heart they hit is, in a real sense, a soul on the road to be saved. And so: amen.

Prayer to Sing on the Beach in Summer

O dear sweet generous Jesus thank you for the sea and the surf and the terns and the pelicans and the sea lions sliding along like small brown buses, and the seals popping up their heads looking like moist Wilford Brimleys, and the seethe and roar and thrum of the sea, and the brilliance of the light, and this most excellent ale in my right hand, and the lanky children skimboarding with startling skill, and the unbelievably lovely woman dozing while pretending to read a novel, and the absence of watches and timepieces and handheld mobile devices, and the lack of things we are supposed to do, and o sweet mother of the mewling baby Jesus, a whale! You are just showing off this afternoon, You and I know that; but no one ever appreciated the show more than me. Thank You. I bow in gratitude. Can You send the whales back this way again? One kid missed the sighting, and it's not every day you see animals the size of school buses in the sea. And so: amen.

Prayer for Miles Davis and Chet Baker

Gentlemen, you did good, even though your lives were tumultuous and confusing and there were brushes with drugs and the law and fisticuffs and bruised feelings among those who loved you best. Still, though—you took the gifts the Conductor gave you and you worked as hard as you could to hone and focus them toward the far frontiers of your ability and the trumpet itself, and it seems to me you got there, not once or twice but a stunning number of times. The accomplishment doesn't excuse the abysmal behavior; but, gentlemen, you made music that has lifted and jazzed millions of hearts, and that is a glorious thing to say, and music is of course the art closest to the heart of the Composer, so this evening, listening to you alternately, I offer a small prayer, with a small whiskey, for the repose of your riveting souls, and for camaraderie in the band in which you now play, and for joy in your unimaginable travels with the Bus Driver. Gentlemen: you did good, and I suspect your music will last on earth as long as human beings yearn and muse and swing and sing. And so: amen.

Prayer for the Silent Man Holding a White Cross in Front of the Building Where We All Know Abortions Are Taking Place

Brother, I respect your quiet insistence on what you believe with all your heart. Brother, I respect your public witness without shrieking or violence. Brother, I too think that we use polite euphemisms for the murder of very small beings. And brother, I too do not know how to forge ahead in any easy way; I too am not a woman and will never be one; so I too do not know the feeling of a child in me, a child I do not want, a child perhaps forced into me against my will; a child where I never wished or expected a child, not now, maybe not ever; a child I view as a stone, an anchor, a drag on who I might be. Yet, brother, I too see a child where some people see a problem, a choice, a decision, a political right; I too think murder is murder, no matter what other words we drape on it to cover the crime; perhaps you too like me think murder is also a good word for war and the poisoning of prisoners, and the deliberate poisoning of rivers and lakes and streams. So a prayer for you, brother, and for me, and for all of us, that we find ways to edge out of our political fortresses, our armed camps, our rock-ribbed convictions, and tiptoe toward shaky common ground, and find ways for children to live; a million new Americans every year, forty million new children in the world every year; who might they be, if they had been allowed to be born? And so: amen.

Prayer for the Immense Woman Who Runs Very Slowly Along the Street Every Morning No Matter What the Weather

You, madame, are a brave and diligent soul, and I admire you very much indeed. You never miss a day that I have noticed. You never quite walk and never quite run, yet you move briskly and relentlessly, and I have seen the pounds melt away, yes I have—at least thirty pounds in the two years I have driven past, impressed and moved, five mornings a week. Your ferocious concentration, looking neither left nor right, ignoring small dogs, dismissing the rain, paying no attention at all to the whippet college students floating past, and the many other morning runners and strollers and bicyclists, and knots of opportunistic crows harvesting shards of squirrel in the cross streets. I pray for your continued energy and willpower. I pray that there is someone or several someones who witness and celebrate and laud your discipline. I pray that you do not stop even when you have attained the weight you want, having discovered the strenuous pleasure of the body moving through the fraught and holy air. I pray for myself that I be granted your steady work ethic and self-discipline, and that I do not flag or surrender when there is work to be done. I pray that I am not the only one who sees you on our street every morning, and that there are many of us whose hearts lift slightly when we see you forging west, patient, graceful, lovely. And so: amen.

Prayer for Boys and Girls of Other Sexual Orientation Than Mine

Brothers and sisters, I did not understand the pain and strain of your lives. I did not know the humiliation you endured. I did not know nor did I even try to know the fear of being cast out from your family and your friends. I did not know what it was like to be insulted and castigated and beaten for the crime of being yourself. I did not know what it was like to be welcomed in word but not in deed in my Church. I did not know the trepidation with which you spoke honestly of who you were for the first time. I did not know nor did I try to know. I made scurrilous remarks myself, once upon a time. I casually tossed slurs for comic effect. I stand here ashamed and abashed. I ask quietly for your forgiveness. I pray for your calm courage and your patience with us who were cruel and dismissive and ignorant and worse. I ask this of the One who once assumed a form like ours, and in that form was insulted and castigated and beaten for the crime of being Himself. I pray that the slow changes I see now in our country and in our species are a sign of our progress another inch toward love; which is why we are here, brothers and sisters. And so: amen.

Prayer for Barry Holstun Lopez, of Finn Rock, Oregon

Who somehow took a childhood of unimaginable fear and pain and milled it into a life of reverence and generosity and attentiveness; who has spent his life listening carefully for the voices of the voiceless, and speaking eloquently and articulately and passionately for them in the public arena; who traveled the world to listen to aboriginal and powerless and ignored people of every color and creed, and returned to his beloved river to write and speak of their concerns and wisdom; who knows that humor is holy and tenderness the greatest of human feats; who is alert to the hand of the Maker in every fish and insect and plant and beast and bird; who took a cornucopia of gifts granted him by the Designer and used them not for gain but as a gift to his companions along the road; for this one smiling bearded man in the wet woods I ask Your blessings this morning, and express gratitude for all Your children who have been elevated by the grace of his company and his prose; he has been a most unusual blessing, Father, for which our most sincere thanks. And so: amen.

Prayer for the Dads Enduring the Epic Winter Rains Along the Muddy Sidelines at Pee Wee Soccer Games

Brothers, I have stood where you stand, in ankle-deep mud, trying not to call instructions and warnings to my child, trying to restrict myself to supportive remarks and not roars of fury at the gangly mute teenage referee who totally missed an assault upon my beloved progeny; and I have also shuffled from leg to leg for an entire hour in an effort to stay warm; and I have also realized I was supposed to bring snacks at halftime five minutes before halftime, and dashed to the store for disgusting liquids in colors unlike any natural color issued from the Creator; and I too have pretended not to care about the score, or about my child's athletic performance, but said cheery nonsense about how I did not care; and I too have resisted the urge to bring whiskey to the game in a thermos, and so battle the incredible slicing wet winds; and I too have resisted the urge to bring the newspaper or a magazine and at least get some reading done during the long periods of languor as small knots of children surround the ball like wolves around a deer and happily kick each other in the shins; and I too have carefully not said a word when my child and six mud-soaked teammates cram into my car and bang out their cleats on my pristine car floor and leave streaks of mud and disgusting plastic juice on the windows; and I too know that this cold wet hour is a great hour, for you are with your child, and your child is happy, and the Coach of all things gave you that child, and soon enough you will be like me, the father of teenagers who no longer stands along the sidelines laughing with the other dads in the rain. Be there now, brothers, and know how great the gift; for everything has its season, and the world spins ever faster. And so: amen.

Prayer for Proofreaders

For your eyesight and your patience, that neither runs out in this lifetime, even though you have to correct the word *hopefully* used at the opening of a sentence for *the one-thousandth time*, but who's bitter? For your meticulous care, that it not turn into mania, and leave you mumbling and gibbering as you walk along the street correcting the names on people's mailboxes and correcting the typos in the newspaper in the office break room and going over old love letters from your wife and making suggested changes in red ink in the margins and then offering them to her for possible updating. For attentiveness to clarity that does not entail wholesale slashing and cutting of entire sections and passages of manuscripts because they do not rise to the level of Robert Louis Stevenson's prose, because who could? For a bemused amusement rather than apoplectic fury when writers do not use the serial comma, or refer to their own experience as ostensible proof and evidence for a thesis, or write nothing but self-absorbed muck, or fawning essays about their satanic cats, or endless lunatic screeds proving beyond the shadow of a doubt that Jesus was Australian. We pray that they never forget that their work finally is for clarity between writer and reader, and that clarity is a blessing, as it brings us closer each to each; which is another aspect of the endless word that is Your love. And so: amen.

Prayer for All the Guys Who Rebounded Shots for Me Over Twenty Years of Basketball

Brothers and friends and guys I never even knew by name who still had the generosity to scour the backboards and whip me the outlet pass without thinking, without reflecting that chances were good they would not see the ball again that play; but still they jockeyed for position amid hips and elbows and shoulders, grabbing and being grabbed, and leapt for the ball, and snagged it, and saw me streaking away, and got me the ball; for your hard work, gentlemen, for your unconscious generosity, for your tumultuous labor, for your adherence to the deep sweet principles of the greatest of games, for your willingness to then follow me down court and many times gather in the rebound on the other end also; for your lack of tart and rude comment when I missed shots, and missed the right pass to you at the right time, and did not use your high pick but unaccountably went the other way, thank you. For your burly cheer and shouldery camaraderie, thank you. For boxing out and opening lanes and setting screens, thank you. For the silent nod back to me when I pointed at you after your rebound led to my easy basket, thank you. For speaking the language of the game we loved, gentlemen, I shout my eternal gratitude; for we were young, we were joyous, we were happy mammals at play; and those were hours I will cherish until the day I die. And so: amen.

Prayer for Good Surfing Conditions This Weekend

I know You have many other much more pressing things to attend to, but if You have a moment to grant miniscule favors, some decent surf for a change would be a real pleasure, as the waves have not been above two feet for two weeks, and my brother and I finally have the hang of the thing after working at it almost every day this summer, and I love hanging around the beach with my brother, for that's when we actually talk about stuff that matters rather than fight and bicker about stuff that doesn't, and it's a clean healthy pursuit too, in which no mind-addling substances are allowed because then you would get muddled and not surf well and end up with your face in the shells at the bottom of the sea, which would be painful not to mention Mom would be mad at the cost of getting your face stitched up right. So, if at all possible, if You can take a second to whip up a small storm fifty miles out, without endangering fishermen, and then send the surf this way on Saturday, we would really appreciate it, and we promise to be there early and surf responsibly and also catch the first Mass on Sunday rather than the Laggard's Mass at noon, like usual. This we pray in the name of Your Son who also, You will remember, walked on water, and so invented surfing, long before Duke Kahanamoku, blessed be his name. And so: amen.

Prayer for My High School History Teacher Mister Shaper

Who taught me that history was not facts and numbers and dates but stories; and that stories were easily remembered and understood; and that if you could share a story then you could connect to someone deeper than the usual business transaction be it sexual or financial or status-jockeying; and that some stories mattered enormously when it comes to figuring out what sort of people and citizens and nations and species we wish to be; and that some American stories were glorious beacons of who we might still someday be, for example Abraham Lincoln boldly making it illegal to sell children according to the colors of their skin ever again in America; and that some American stories ought to be remembered forever as occasions of terrible shame and sin, for example our massacre of hundreds of innocent helpless Filipino women and children on the island of Jolo in 1906, or our massacre of hundreds of innocent helpless American women and children at Wounded Knee Creek in 1890, because to forget murder was to open the door for it to crawl sneering and leering into the world again, riding on carpets of lies. So a prayer for Mister Shaper, small and round and smiling and brilliant and patient beyond belief with his gawkish charges; a prayer for his peace and serenity, wherever he is today in the world You made; and grant him an instant of unaccountable satisfaction about his teaching career, let it flood into his day with no warning, such that he grins and thinks *now where did* that *come from?* And so: amen.

Prayer for My Man Daniel Age Three Who Will Die from Cancer in About Two Weeks

And knows it, too, but doesn't complain. And he's in ferocious pain. But he just takes it. His father is a huge guy who cries every time he starts to say something about the courage and grace and guts of his son. His mother just holds him and runs her hand over his hands. There's nothing to be done anymore. My man Daniel doesn't have hardly any hair anymore. His eyes are huge. My man Daniel wanted to be a firefighter. The firefighters in his town wear helmets with his photograph on them. The firefighters in his town made Daniel an honorary member of their firehouse. There's a locker in the house for his coat and helmet. When they talk about him they say *Daniel our brother* and they say *his duty shift is about to end*. They asked other fire stations around the world to make Daniel a firefighter too and dozens of stations in America and Canada and Australia did that immediately, and lots of those stations gave him a locker in their stations also, with his name above his locker. After Daniel dies in about two weeks the firefighters in his town will still wear their helmets for another year or two or three, I bet. So that when those guys go to save someone's life Daniel will be there with them somehow. I don't know how Daniel can be there and not be there. But *You* do. I don't know anything this morning except how to weep for my man Daniel and his poor mom and dad and those poor brave tall sturdy tree-trunk firefighters who will sob like babies in their firehouse pretty soon. But *You* know my man Daniel and his brothers at the firehouse. Deluge them with the cataclysm of Your love? And so: amen.

Prayer for the Elderly Woman on the Train Eating One Almond Every Five Minutes for Two Hours for a Grand Total of Forty Almonds and Believe Me I Counted, Fascinated

Partly because she was about eight inches away from me and the intricate process of getting the bag of almonds *out* of her vast carryall and then choosing *exactly* the *right* one and then chewing *that single almond* as carefully and slowly as any being has ever in this blessed world chewed a single nut back to individual atoms is driving me quietly bonkers; but I am fascinated too because she has slowly and silently reminded me not to be an arrogant idiot. Maybe this is all the food she has for her journey. Maybe she is a bodhisattva who is trying to remind me to savor every instant of this wild and lovely life. Maybe she is a saint who is saying to me gently, *Assume nothing, the exterior is a disguise and a costume, and I am a holy being also formed by the Imaginative One, and here we are together, younger brother, on a train with almonds! Are we not blessed? Are we not graced beyond words that no one is shooting at us, and we are rushing magically through the countryside without effort, and our bellies are not shriveled from starvation, and we are alive and breathing and there is the redolence of almonds between us?* And these things are true and she is right and I grin and feel a tinge of regret when she finishes the bag, which must have contained exactly forty almonds; did she count them out one by one last night, staring intently at the small russet oblong glory of each, before sealing the bag? So then I pray for each of us, that we stare intently at the wilderness of miracles around us every moment, so very many of them savory. And so: amen.

Prayer for All Saints and All Souls Day

And if ever there was evidence of the wry genius of Catholicism it's right here, with these two days of prayer and remembrance, back to back. The first acknowledges, up front and publicly, that we pray for saints known and unknown—the latter faaaaar outnumbering the former; and how true and real and honest this is, for there are and have been millions of saints who trudged along humbly beneath immense loads, sharing their mercy and cheer and song and food and drink and courage and hope with everyone they met, and now their names are as dust; but we remember them today, and thank them, and ask their mercies on the tumult of the world; as we sing also the saints we know, the brave testy ones, the quiet ones who smiled under the lash, the bold ones who saw what we could be and spoke us closer to that bright country. And then the next day we pray for all those who have gone back into the Dream from which they came, all the billions of holy beings who strove and struggled and soared or sank; all of them our brothers and sisters, all of them our teammates on the road to light; we pray even for the worst among them, those blinded by blood, that Your mercy drowned their evil, washed them of their sins, and set them to work in Your vineyard, from which all blessings flow. This we pray in the Name of the One Who came among us, and took our form, and draped His incomprehensible soul with the flesh and bones of a young teacher; may we someday reach the house where He waits for us all. And so: amen.

Prayer of Gratitude & Awe for the Lanky Silent Genius Informational Technology Guy Who Just Fixed My Computer by Glaring at It & Waving His Hand

And then nodded politely at me and vanished. You wouldn't believe how quick and efficient and deft and un-arrogant this kid was, and he looked to be about nine years old, although he had one of those awful chin-sprout goatees like strands of seaweed growing out of his face. He was on time, he asked me penetrating questions about the disaster and did not flinch when I used rude and vituperative language about the defiant machine, and then he sat down for forty seconds and instantly diagnosed and solved the problem. Nor did he then sneer at me for being a dolt, or crow over his triumph, or do a little victory dance while singing some horrifying modern music; he stood up, offered me my chair courteously, gave me his card with a direct phone access in case of further questions, and slid away silently. We never say thanks enough for people who can do well the things that we cannot even imagine doing poorly; but this morning, for a moment, you and me together, standing closely but not holding hands or any of that sort of thing, should do so. And so: amen.

Prayer of Gratitude for Weekday Noon Masses

Which were clearly, bless their inventors, designed for working people, designed for men and women and kids who want a little jolt of elevation and epiphany and Eucharist and camaraderie and contemplation in the middle of the workday, designed for those who wish to sip a little sacrament as a pause or respite or revival amid hours of whatever labor it is they do. This is just raw sweet honest human *genius*, the noon Mass. This is not the sprawl of Sunday Mass, which can, let us be honest, often lumber and wheeze, and on some occasions is more pomp and performance than it is lean holy meal with piercing stories. No, the workday Mass is stripped to its essentials—stories, miracle, Communion, go ye and be the Word of the Lord. We pause, for a moment, outside the chapel doors, and shake hands, and blink in the unexpected sunlight, and feel a little . . . what? cleaner? taller? refreshed? centered? balanced? lighter of spirit? And away we go in the four holy directions, back to offices and work-rooms and cubicles and shops and stations and piers

and counters and convents, somehow gently better.
What a sweet subtle gift that I hope we never take for
granted. And so: amen.

Prayer of Reluctant Grumpy Disgruntled Moist Thanks for Steady Winter Rain

Listen, I know I would be crowing with delight if I were a farmer or a vineyard owner, and I would be beaming with pleasure if I ran a ski shop, because of course up in the mountains this is all snow, and all the water-resource professionals are gibbering with joy because we are filling reservoirs and stashing summer rivers as winter snowpacks, but I am just a guy down in the valley and it has been raining steadily since Lincoln was president, and I am wet and weary and weary of wet. My shoes are soggy, my jacket is moist, my cap has shrunk a size from all the soaking and then steaming dry by the fire, my pants have permanent jagged marks from a thousand splashes, the dog will never be fully dry ever again . . . but I know this is clean free glorious generous water falling from the sky, and clean water is the story of the future of the world, and I love this world, and love that this water will fill children with the best food of all, and I know we are mostly water, and that in the end this is the sweetest gift of the physical world, along with miraculous air and the seethe of soil beneath our feet; so I curtail the moaning, and shuffle along trying to avoid the larger seas in the pavement, and thank You; but tonight yes I will go through my photographs from last summer, yearning a little, okay? No disrespect. And so: amen.

Prayer for the Teenage Girl Singing with All Her Might as She Stands Alone at the Bus Stop

Bring it and sing it, kid. Rip it and roar it. Life's short and you should sing with all your might when you get the chance especially if no sneery kids who think they are too cool to sing are glaring at you or making scurrilous remarks. Bellow and blare it. People who think they are too cool to sing are not cool at all. People who *sing* are cool. People who don't sing because they think their voice stinks are fools to worry about what other people think. Who cares what other people think about your voice? Voices are like women; they're all lovely. Even low muttery growls and cracked atonal off-key bleats are lovely. *Singing* is lovely. Singing is praying with your mouth. Singing is what we do to say thanks for the breath that spins into song. Singing is how the universe came into being. In the beginning was the Singing. You can hear it still everywhere if you listen. I heard it this morning at the bus stop. I have been singing the rest of the day. I sing like a rock rolling downhill, I sound like a whale with the flu, but I am singing because you sang with all your might, kid. Thank you for reminding me to rip it and roar it. And so: amen.

Prayer of Gratitude for the Chicago White Sox

In the aggregate, I guess—the *idea* of the Sox, not any specific amalgam, although I know You and I both have a soft spot in our hearts for the 1977 club, with Richie Zisk and Chet Lemon and Oscar Gamble, o my gawd that foot-high afro, how that man kept his hat on when he ran is a mystery to me. No, I offer this smiling prayer for the Soxness of the Sox—their awful seasons, their cheerful motley fans, the way we all ambled and shambled toward the park in the afternoon as if it were an enormous magnet, which it was; the *companionship* of it all, the folks sitting near you who said *hey* and *what's up* and *want a beer*, the way those few fans who were there savored and celebrated the moments when the sun dissolved and the lights snapped on, and the shocking sudden triple lashed into the gap, and the occasional unbelievable play that no one could remember ever having seen before; the smells and sounds of a city evening in America, the swifts overhead, the faint thunder of trains, the swelling roar as we realized what had happened half a second before down on the green jewel of the field; the timelessness of it, the slouched pleasure, the hard seats, the laughter as we crammed back into the train; for all the nonsense ever written about baseball, there is and was so much sweet gentle communal pleasure and grace and generosity; and for that, this hot summer evening, listening to nighthawks, I thank You. And so: amen.

Prayer of Gratitude for the Doctor Who Saved My Son

It's awfully tempting to think, sometimes, that You made him just for this purpose, hatching him in California and defending him against his own headlong idiocy long enough to get him trained as a cardiologist, and making sure he didn't break his neck with his madcap skiing, or die young because he worked twenty hours a day and hardly slept, or grew dark and weary after thousands of broken children were carried into his office by parents so frightened and desperate they could hardly speak; but I know You let him form inside his cool brave tiny mother because You foment countless miracles like that every moment, and that is Your job, fomenting miracles, like the imagining of this universe, for example, well done there by the way; and I suspect You let Dave find his own way in the world because that is our job, thrashing toward light and humility and tenderness and creativity, and losing our egos along the way if we are wise; but I am awfully glad You fomented the particular miracle named Dave, because he then used his capacious imagination and skill to save my son's life, my son who would have died at age seven without Dave, my son who is not dead, not today, and I know this because I just had my hand on his shoulder a moment ago; as I pray You will always have Your hand there too; and on Dave's shoulder, as a proud father salutes a son; for he did well, Father; believe me, he did real well. And so: amen.

Prayer of Awed Thanks for Nurses

Witnesses, attendants, bringers of peace; brilliant technical machinists; selfless cleaners of all liquids no matter how horrifying; deft finders of veins when no veins seem available; soothers and calmers and amusers; tireless and patient and tender souls; brisk and efficient when those are the tools to keep despair at bay; those with prayers in their mouths as their patients slide gently though the mysterious gate, never to return in a form like the shriveled still one in the bed; feeders and teasers, mercies and singers; they who miss nothing with their eyes and ears and fingers and hearts; they who are not saluted and celebrated and worshipped as they ought to be; they who are the true administrators of hospitals and clinics, for it is they who have their holy hands on the brows and bruises of the broken and frightened; they who carry the new infants to their sobbing exhausted thrilled mothers; they who must carry the news of damage and death to the family in the waiting room; they whom You know, each and every one, glorious and lovely in their greens and blues and rainbow clothing; they who are You in every tender touch and quiet friendly gentle murmured remark; they who are the best of us; bless them always and always,

Mercy; for they are the clan of calm and the tribe of tender, and I bow in thanks for them. And so: amen.

Prayer for the Commonwealth of Australia

That it be a nation that gets it all right, for once; that edges away from its violent past and act of original theft, and sings and supports its First Peoples; that it be a nation that edges away from marking people by the shade of their skin, but counts them instead as citizens or friends; that it stands ever tall and stalwart against aggression and greed, but uses its stunning creativity and humor to find and wield new weapons that shed no blood and leave no children sobbing; that it not pillage its own land and water for mere money, but conserve and protect the gifts You gave it for all generations to come; that I stand alongside its friends among other nations, and convert its enemies by the substance of its character and the honesty of its dealings; that it eject the liars and thieves among its leaders, and seek among its populace men and women who lead with vision married to humility; that it be a land open to new citizens fleeing murderous thugs, and by its welcome turn its new citizens into eloquent agents for freedom and responsibility; that it mill its famous humor and courage into a new sort of nation, where independence and interdependence are lovers, and not false enemies; we pray this in Your names, of which there are and have been so very many, in so many languages, in so many million mouths. And so: amen.

Prayer to Assuage the Loneliness of Priests & Nuns & Brothers

Brothers and sisters, I remember a wise priest telling me this: Celibacy is not the problem; loneliness is the problem. This resonates with me still, my friends, and I offer a prayer to fend off long afternoons when no one speaks to you and you speak to no one, to fend off empty mailboxes, to fend off your birthday sliding by without comment, to fend off days when a terse argument with a comrade is the best conversation of the day. I pray that solitude is refreshing and not crushing. I pray that you have fifty sons and daughters if you count the children of people who admire and respect you. I pray that every child you baptize or teach or minister to considers you an aunt or an uncle of a sort. I pray that you have friends in every walk of life who send you notes and buy you pints and ask your counsel in matters not religious as well as of course spiritual conundrums. I pray that you have buddies for chess and river walking and bird-watching and coffee klatsching and watching crucial second-round playoff games. I pray that the people you meet in the social ramble light up when they see you approaching. I pray all these things in the name of the One who is our first and greatest friend. And so: amen.

Prayer for the Soul of the Late James Naismith, of Ontario, Canada

Because he is famous for one thing we forget he was a real man, struggling and brave. We forget he was an orphan whose parents both died of fever when he was nine. We forget he was a poor student who willed himself to be better and eventually graduated from college with honors. We forget he was a terrific athlete himself, one of the best in his new nation. We forget that his superior gave him only two weeks to invent a new game, and that rather than dive in blindly or copy other games he sat and thought carefully about flow and joy. His first principles for his new game were that there would be no deliberate violence, as in football and rugby; that the ball would be large and relatively soft, unlike the stony pellets of baseball and hockey; and that the goal would not be obstructed by a keeper, further reducing collisions and the loss of teeth. The game would reward deft and graceful motion, not brawn; creativity would trump size and aggression; sleight of hand would be rewarded, and assault punished. The game would be fast and vigorous, with a minimum of contact, and it could be played indoors or out. Thus, in the winter of 1891, in a gym in Massachusetts, a man just turned thirty years old invented basketball, the greatest of all games, the most liquid and generous of them all; and this morning, watching my sons stretching for their game in a moment, I thank You for inventing Jimmy Naismith, who made the world a better place. And so: amen.

Prayer for My Boys, the Priests & Brothers of the Congregation of Holy Cross in the United States

Brothers, I have seen, with high glee, your dopey mistakes and foolish stumbles; and I have also seen your courage and grace and generosity and kindness and wisdom; and to my amazement I have to say that the latter far outweigh the former, as far as I can see, in my forty years of walking the road with you; and this is an astonishing thing to say of any human entity, particularly one sworn to work that doesn't make money or earn you fame or cool cars. Indeed you are sworn agents of the wild idea that light defeats darkness and hope hammers despair, when we know the evidence is everywhere to the contrary; yet you persist, mostly making wise decisions and keeping your egos the size of acorns and pebbles. Mostly you are the best priests and brothers I ever saw, listening patiently to kids as their hearts break and open and shiver and expand; mostly you never forget that you are just as capable of genius and idiocy as we layfolk are; and even though you are sworn never to have lovers, sworn to obey the very authority you might want to occasionally hit with a small mammal, sworn to forswear the trappings of power and pride, you carry these unusual weighted vows with humor and wit and patience and grace. Brothers, I repeat, you amaze me; and I ask the One to bless you always, to give you strength and endurance for your hard road, to soothe your souls when you are weary, and to give you the wisdom to seek always for humility—the final frontier, and the open door to His house. And so: amen.

Snarling Prayer for the Reckless Jerk Who Just Swerved Insanely Among Three Lanes of Traffic at Incredible Speed *While Texting,* Causing Us Other Drivers Heart Palpitations

You are important and we are not. *You* ought not to be slowed down by cars in your way, because you are you and we are only dross and froth. *You* obviously are a terrific driver, cool as you text behind the wheel of your shining new Lexus, and we are merely drivers of battered ancient wagons that should be recycled into recalcitrant toasters. Really we should have pulled to the side of the road and gaped as you whizzed by, but forgive us for not realizing immediately you were so cool. Now we know, and as soon as my heart rate retreats and my fingers unclench from the steering wheel and my rage begins to subside and the visions I had of smoking wrecks and sobbing children dissolve, I will offer a disgruntled prayer for you, you selfish fool: that you get a grip, that you see what fear and turmoil you put into people's hearts when you drive like that, that you get a dose of humility without paying for it in your blood or someone else's. I pray also that you soon get the biggest speeding ticket in the history of the state of Oregon, so big it has its own zip code. I pray you have an epiphany and realize you are not actually the most important or interesting person on the planet. I pray that you grow up. It took me long enough to begin to grow up, so I am not crowing here; I'm just saying I hope the One gently delivers a message to you soon, before you kill yourself or someone else, you arrogant dolt. And so: amen.

Prayer of Gratitude That There Are Newts in This World

Because, c'mon, wouldn't it be less of a cool world if there were no newts? And tree frogs? And pipits and damselflies? And kindergarten kids on rainy days with every color and style of rubber rain boot you can imagine? And Van Morrison? And parrots and herons? And teachers who look at kids and see that they have not slept right because their gramma just died and the teacher gives the kid an extra two days to turn in the paper but doesn't make a big deal out of it? And priests who don't give you advice but just listen? And cheese sandwiches and tea when you have walked for five miles in the wet woods up and down through ravines and thickets and meadows and copses and tangles and you stop for a late lunch, and isn't that the best thing you ever ate in your life and whoever invented hot tea with honey is a saint? And mockingbirds and news-papers and godparents and ale? And ponytails and pigtails and crew cuts, and turquoise earrings worn by women with piercing laser eyes so bright that they ought to have to get permits for their use in the day-time? And footballs and teenagers and rivers roaring with snowmelt? Am I right? Do we ever stop and pray enough for the wealth of small things that are not small at all? We do not. But we do now. And so: amen.

Prayer of Thanks for the Man or Woman or Child Who Invented Socks

Probably from grass or rushes or tree fibers, in the beginning. Maybe his or her sandals were wearing out, and growing so thin you could almost see through them, and he or she made a new pair, and slipped them on over the old pair, and the light went on! And all the other people in the tribe gawked and said us too man! And there was a run on fibers and rushes and other stuff you could weave into rough socks! And then people began to experiment with the skins of animals and seaweed and fern fronds and banana leaves, and with a little infinitesimal shiver history spun a bit, and socks became normal, and words were invented for this cool new thing, and eventually the Greeks used the word *sukkhos*, which became the Roman *soccus*, which became the Anglo *socc*, which became the lovely warm black basketball socks I stole from my second son this morning, on the theory that *I* was up and off to work and *he* would not even think of socks until noon. So, Lord, my most sincere thanks; and a prayer too on the sleeping boy. And so: amen.

Prayer for My College Roommates

Brothers, I wish you well, and ask the mercy and humor of the Lord upon your days and works, even though you never hung up those wet towels, and you played that awful Peter Frampton music incessantly until there was that incident for which I am marginally sorry even today, and you did inflict that weird blue wood paneling on the room, and you did totally dominate the phone calling your high-school girlfriend eighteen hours a day, and you did practice your Shakespeare monologues aloud at three in the morning until I was ready to shriek and rend my shirt if I ever again heard Lear moaning and complaining in the upper bunk, and you did force me to read and edit your papers on Kierkegaard and Nietzsche and Proust even though I was clear that I could not bear any of the three of those self-absorbed brilliances and would have happily sent them to sea together for months at a time on seal-hunting expeditions in the Arctic, all three of them could have used a little fresh air and exercise to clear their minds; yet I have the utmost affection and respect for you, brothers, and wish you well, and ask the blessings of the One on your motley journeys and misadventures. And so: amen.

Prayer of Thanks for Iowa

Which hatched James Norman Hall and Wallace Stegner, great American writers, and Greg Brown and Art Farmer, great American musicians, and Herbert Hoover, who saved millions of people from starving, and Donna Reed, who was blessedly Donna Reed, and Billy Sunday, who tried to bring light to darkness, and Bob Feller, the Heater from Van Meter . . . but any and all states can claim famous nativities. No, let us pause this morning and thank the Governor of all things for the soil and water and green and gentle of Iowa, for its whirling snow and smiling citizens, for its rolling cropland and occasional copses of trees, for its bobcats and turtles, for its First Peoples resident and migrant there ten thousand years ago, for the zest with which Iowans savor being first to vote for a new American president, for its wrestling and basketball prowess, for its lack of civil arrogance and pomposity, for the great wide epic American river that flows along its eastern border. We read casually about Iowa; we hear the word occasionally like a snippet of song; we know it is there, calm and dignified in the American midst; but we do not say thanks enough for the Iowaness of it; so for that, and especially for Donna Reed, thank You. And so: amen.

Prayer for Sisters Generally Also Known as Nuns (of All Religions)

Because those are the coolest bravest most humble most relaxed and funny religious people there are. Fact. Because they are in my experience the most humble and amused religious people I ever saw. Because they have never been charged with thousands of rapes worldwide. Because they generally abjure power, as far as I can tell. Because they have happily changed with the times and they come out from their convents and cloisters and stay focused on Jesus's original mission statement better than any other religious people I ever saw. Because they are generally brilliant but do not think they are cool. Because the best of them have said to me, when I ask about the precipitous decline in vocations among them, *it's not a disaster, it's a great opportunity for new work!* Because it seems to me we Catholics trust and admire nuns more than any other religious people I know. Because like priests and brothers they took the original mission statement so to heart that they swore and vowed their lives in service to it, which is amazing and astonishing and we do not sing and celebrate that enough. But let us do so, this morning. And so: amen.

Quiet Prayer for Friends Whose Teenage Child Just Stormed Out of the House

Cursing and spitting and smashing a plate along the way, for effect. Slapped the mother twice as hard as possible and would have slapped the father too except the other child stepped in and hustled the first child out in the yard where there was a tumult and then the first child ran away down the street and the second child came back in the house pale and drawn and furious and afraid. No one said anything for a few minutes. O God help them tonight and tomorrow and next year. Ease the savage stab of the insults and screaming and slapping and fear and rage and pain. Heal them sometime somehow somewhere with Your mercy. We have so many of us been in that kitchen with rage and blood and violence in the air. Yes, we have. We don't talk about this much except to You in the dark reaches of the night. O God help them come through this somehow. I don't see how. But You do, don't You? Don't You? I am not asking for You to make everything better; I am only asking You to lead them to the strength and humility to reach for each other again somehow sometime and to try to build little rickety bridges. I know how You work; the best in us is another word for You. May they somehow open the bruised treasures of the best of themselves, and reach for each. I cannot see how they can do that, after what just happened; but You do. Lean toward them today? Please? And so: amen.

Prayers for the Soul of the Late Karol Józef Wojtyła of Poland

Listen, Lord, can we talk directly here, man to Creator? You have a guy back home there with You who did great things and foolish things when he was here, and back here we are insulting him with mere hagiography, and I want to set the record straight and salute what he did well, while sighing at his blinkered mistakes. He never did get it that women are incredible resources in the Church and ought to be promoted to every position of power and authority. He was wildly inconsistent about totalitarianism, fighting it with courage and wit in Europe and preventing its toppling in Latin America. He never did do much about thousands of children being raped in the Church, although there's no way he didn't have an inkling of it. On the other hand, he was the first pope ever to kneel down and apologize for the many sins of the Church, and he was the first one to apologize to Your chosen people the Jews for the Church's awful abuse of them over the centuries, and he was the first one to bow in prayer at the Wailing Wall in Jerusalem, and he visited and forgave the idiot who tried to kill him, and there's no question that his verve and courage and humor elevated and inspired the lives and days of millions of people around the world. So will You do me a favor, and tell him we miss him, and admire him, and celebrate him in all his muddleheadedness and grace? We just officially formally learnedly named him a saint; but many of us will better remember the real guy, who was, like us, capable of both heroism and idiocy. And so: amen.

Prayer for the Incredibly Loud Recycling Truck That Comes at Dawn Every Thursday Morning

Which thank God it does, for can you *believe* we used to throw all that stuff out? Those groaning barrels of paper and cardboard and plastic and glass and lawn clippings and dead fronds from the cedar and fir trees? But every Thursday morning at dawn or sometimes before dawn here comes that vast epic roaring truck, and I lie abed and listen as the guys leap off from where they are hanging on the sides, and they chaff each other as they haul buckets, and then the truck uses its vast arm to pick up the biggest bucket and flip it, and there's a huge crash as everything lands amidships, and then the truck grumbles on down the hill (I can hear the gears shifting if I listen sharp) and every time I think, Lord, thanks for those guys, and keep their backs strong, and thanks for giving us the wit to finally realize we cannot continue to trash the world You dreamed into being. Thanks for giving us the brains to begin to figure out ways to stop committing the sin of stealing clean air and clean water from our children. And I pray quietly, as I get up and ponder the miracle of coffee, that it is not too late for us to clean the miracle You handed us like a glowing green jewel, so long ago. And so: amen.

Prayer for Cats

Look, Lord, You and I know they are a sneering super-cilious arrogant species, more than willing to defile shoes and bite the hands that feed them, and they seem oily and fatuous and pompous to me, happy only when beheading innocent birds or eviscerating harmless tiny mammals or ignoring the human servants who gener-ally are only looking for a little affection and company in exchange for all the money and time they lavish upon haughty cats, despite the stench and disdain of the lat-ter; but there must be some redeeming virtue in them, or they would not have bloomed into being after You set the worlds to spin and the stars to burn; so with total confusion as to what conceivable virtue they might possess, with a smidgen of grudging admiration for their lithe athleticism, and with the deep conviction that there must be something good about cats that I will never see, I offer thanks for whatever it is You had in mind there, and reflect that this very conviction that there must be something there that I will never under-stand is an excellent blunt lesson in what the word *faith* means. And so: amen.

Absolutely Serious Prayer in Celebration of Port-A-Potties

Because someone *made* them, am I right? Someone worked hard on their design, and manufacture, and delivery, and installation, and maintenance, and we never say thanks for that, for the hard work those men and women do, for the way their work supports their families, for the way their salaries help pay for schools and firemen and policemen and clean water in their towns and cities. Like we never really say thanks and ask for the blessings of the One on janitors and housekeepers and late-night cleaning crews and hotel maids, who work awfully hard to clean that which we barely notice is clean, but if it wasn't clean we would be whining and complaining and leaving tart messages for someone, am I right? So a prayer for the health and safety and peace of those who clean and scrub, those who design and build and distribute and keep clean the machines that we all use all the time but hardly ever connect to brave holy beings. And so: amen.

Prayer on Father's Day

Brothers, I too have spent many sleepless hours worrying about money and insurance and minor-in-possession citations and speeding tickets and endless bouts of the flu which might mean some horrifying disease. I too have snarled and barked and growled and roared at my children. I too have sometimes, usually in the shower, wondered what crimes I committed in a previous life to be afflicted so with rude and surly and vulgar and unappreciated progeny. Yet I too, brothers, know that they are why we are the luckiest men who ever lived; and I too have laughed so hard at their capers and antics that I had to lie down for a while; and I too have bathed and fed and rocked and coddled and wrestled and played and sung with them, and believed myself at those moments to be closer to heaven than any man ever, and known that this was indeed so, even more than it was and is in the delightful throes of romantic love. So, brothers, a prayer for us today, as we are handed useless garish neckties and Weedwackers that will soon rust and die in the shed, and scrawled coupons for chores to be done in the future; for we are blessed, brothers, and we know it in our better moments, and we pray that today is composed of only those, for once. And so: amen.

Prayer for the Brave Small Girl Who Had the Courage to Ask Me *What Is Wrong with Your Nose, Mister?*

A question she explained helpfully was occasioned by the loud honking droning sound I make at the end of sentences, and by the way it has lumps and bumps in it, sir. After I stop laughing and remembering my brothers calling me Beak as a boy I explain that my nose, never petite to begin with, was then amended over the years by brothers, one of whom broke my nose with a large piece of wood, and by basketball opponents, two of whom broke my nose with their elbows, so that my nose, epic from birth, then added ridges of scar tissue and stuff like that, which is probably why I sound like a truck backing up, or a goose with a sinus condition, or a walrus early in the morning before he's had coffee. On the way home from the grade school I grin for a while and then I feel a surge of affection for this sweet honest kid, all of eight years old; keep this kid curious and open and unadorned forever, maybe? Keep her eager funny spirit untrammeled and unafraid? And maybe give us a reminder of how wild and holy that open curiosity is in this life, if we have lost its zest and spice in our latter years? And so: amen.

Prayer of Intercession for Jorge Mario Bergoglio

Lord, thanks first of all for the humility of the guy. Any guy who says *who am I to judge?* is a guy with his head on straight, a guy who gets it that whatever you are absolutely arrogantly sure of you ought not to be, and that You are the only One who is absolutely sure about things; the rest of us muddle along, dimly shuffling toward the light, mostly. And a guy who is suspicious of power and wealth and its trappings and prisons—that's a good guy. A guy who when asked who he is says first *I am a sinner*—that's a guy with his ego in proportion to his confidence. A guy who quietly turns the ship back toward its original destination, dealing with the broken Christ in every single one of us, rather than continuing along with power and pronouncements—that's a good guy. A prayer for the peace and health of the man, that slimeballs addicted to power and money don't drag him down. A prayer for him that he continues to foment a quiet revolution against wealth and power and arrogance and lies. A prayer that he remembers it's all about kids and the Church ought to be ashamed to its bones for the rest of its life on earth for kids being raped in its house and men lying about it for years afterward. A prayer that he never gets cocky and always remembers we are a cult of countercultural revolutionaries, agents for life, agents for crazy hope, agents for resurrections in *this* life, in our hearts and marriages and families and friendships. A prayer that he steers us ever away from being a huge corporation and ever back to the motley community of believers in the defiantly unreasonable and illogical and nonsensical. Keep Your hand on this guy, please Lord? Protect him from his enemies, and help him quietly gather us back together in work that matters, not in silly arguments. And so: amen.

Prayer for the Publishers of Catholic Books

Brothers and sisters, you are brave mammals. You insist on a world where people share stories and search sometimes desperately for stories that *matter*, stories that are food for the quailing spirit. You are crazy people by the usual calculations; you will never be rich; you will lie awake and worry about small profits and large inventories; you will be afflicted by hirsuited authors who detest being edited; you will dicker and bicker with the printer and the distribution company; you will endure the slings and arrows of lunatic readers aghast that your books do not feature enough paintings of simpering angels with haircuts like Prince Valiant; you will hear tart remarks from the hierarchy occasionally about the way your books are after the genius of Catholicism rather than merely lauding the robed powers that be; you will suffer a few books returned because there is a word misspelled on page 145; you will endure manuscript submissions from people who can prove beyond the shadow of a doubt that all religions were invented by otters in Morocco, or that Jesus did not die but went on to a long career in cricket, or that Saint Catherine of Siena was actually a hop farmer named Herman; reviewers will misunderstand your books, and marginalize them, and booksellers will accidentally file them as fantasy fiction; yet you persist, day after day, because you know that hitting hearts is the point, the work, the reward. I ask the blessings of the One upon you; and ask the Publisher of all things for rivers of peace and joy in your days. And so: amen.

Prayer for Protestants of Every Tradition

How tempting to say bluntly here, what is it you are Protesting against now? The vast bloody greedy corporation that was the Catholic Church centuries ago is no more; we no longer conduct wars, or sell coupons to heaven, or murder our enemies, or run other nations from behind the robes of kings. This is not to say we have no flaws; but are our flaws so unlike those in your tradition? Could it not be that the time has come, as the late John Paul II himself suggested, that we join forces again under the flag of the Judean rabbi? We apologize for our sins; we admit that Martin Luther was right; we remind you Anglicans that you were Catholic before an English king cast lustful eyes elsewhere than he should, and bent a religion to his purposes; we wonder with affection and respect and reverence for your grace and creativity, if there's a way for us all to gather back under the same huge tent; we note that if we did so there would be some two billion of us, which is a remarkable number of people devoted to peace and mercy and service to the Christ in every heart; and even as we acknowledge the thorny theological and logistical issues, we ask politely that at least for the next few minutes you ponder this: What if? And so: amen.

Prayer on Easter Morning

Yes, my *mind* knows that this is clearly riffing on ancient rebirth rituals to honor life returning from what was seemingly forever dead and icy and lifeless ground; and yes, my *mind* savors the genius of Christianity, happily surfing on prehistoric human ceremonies, how deft we are in our appropriation, taking only the best; and my *mind* knows full well that Jesus very probably arose from the dead on a Tuesday afternoon at happy hour, rather than a Sunday morning; yet my heart leaps, and my soul is delighted, and my mouth is filled with joy, for Easter is undeniably the coolest of our annual high holy days, the day when that which we believe unbelievably to be true is shouted from churches and chapels around the world, in every language, by people of every age from small children capering in their annual finery to the ancients who sit and grin at the swirl and song of it all, and then shuffle to the banquet table. This is the day when we admit, smiling, that the essence of our faith doesn't make sense and isn't physically possible; how great and brave is that? How refreshing, to not make sense for once, how refreshing to remember that we are sworn to live by our conviction that there is so much more beyond sense! And so: amen.

Prayer for Catherine Astrid Salome Freeman of Queensland, Australia

Because your parents divorced when you were five years old. Because your sister died when you were eighteen. Because your brother died not long after that. Because the First Peoples in your country were hunted and shot and massacred by people who stole their land and their livelihood and their dignity, and you are one of them, but you would not accept the loss, and used the gifts the One gave you to win races, and run like the breeze through the bushlands, and speak clearly and honestly and bluntly your opinions of mistreatment of First Peoples. Because you had the gall and the temerity and the courage and the roaring insistence on justice and free speech to carry not only the flag of your native country but also the flag of your broken and scattered people when you won your Olympic gold medal, and there are millions of people who watched that moment, weeping with admiration and some deep wriggle of awe, and I am among them, Cathy Freeman. So a prayer for you and your children and your people, that they will ever be in the light of the Imagination that made all things; and my thanks that you are among those things, and I was granted the eyes to see your grace and heart. And so: amen.

Prayer for Sacristans & Altar Societies & Deacons & Church Janitors & Carpenters

Brothers and sisters, if not for you we would not have the thrill and theater of the Mass, and that would be a terrible loss, for the access to miracle every blessed day (twice a day, if you want) is a crucial touchstone for our faith, and a Mass is performance and ambiance and redolence and angles of light and the creak of pews and magician's gesture and camaraderie in the audience, along with being a silent vehicle for miracle and communion and meditation and refreshment; so for your clean cloths and well-made joists, your woven vestments and your clean windows, your beautifully built altar and candles that smell like spring and grandmothers, your quiet service to the faithful even when you have many other things to do that might even pay unlike your work for us, I offer this prayer of thanks; may the Celebrant keep you always in the unimaginable chapel of His heart; as you are in ours, even though we don't tell you that, much. And so: amen.

Prayer of Gratitude for Small Things Done Very Well That You Only Notice When You Sit Still & Pay Attention

Like for example the meticulous tile work in the men's room of the office building; somebody worked hard and well here, when he could so easily have been a little sloppy and filled in the mistakes with glutinous glop; but he didn't. Or the beautifully made sandwich, cut with care, presented with a smile, when it would have been so easy to just slap it together and plop it on the counter without a glance at the customer. Or the wonderful silence as the priest listens without editorial comment or flip advice or packaged wisdom or rote response to the confessor pouring her heart out even though he wants to shriek at what she has done and failed to do; but because he does not issue pompous or even humble comment, she is not dammed, but unburdens and opens and is refreshed simply by the flood, which is a crucial part of the sacrament. Or the way someone just gets up gently silently from the table and slides away and accomplishes the dishes while the headlong burble at the table continues so that when everyone gets up there's not much else to be done; that is grace. The carefully vacuumed carpet, the manicured sand of prayer gardens and golf courses, the perfectly made bed, the sharpened pencils before the exam, the button sewn back on without a trace of repair, the shining windows of the chapel . . . for these and all else of this ilk our prayers of thanks; for those who make these things happen, thanks; for You who made all manner of things well, thanks. And so: amen.

Prayer of Awed Admiration for the Islands of Hawai'i

Look, I know that there are more extraordinarily beautiful and redolent and peaceful and lush and bracing places on this wild earth than anyone but You knows, and I know Hawai'i has its problems with pollution and drugs and crime and corruption and the theft of land and water from a free and independent people many years ago, but I have to say that *I* personally cannot imagine that there is a cooler place in the world than Hawai'i. I mean, here You were working with all Your skills in full flower—a real exercise in creative mastery. I say this with reverence. The epic mountains and the thrilling forests, the joyous music and the generous people, the incredible ocean everywhere singing and lashing the volcanic land, the stupendous bird life, the monk seals like large snoring uncles on the beach; whew. Listen, I know You get a lot of plaudits for design and manufacture and systems engineering, and I know they are well earned, and I know You have heard *a lot* of compliments on this particular project, but I just got there finally in recent years, after fifty years of dreaming about it, and I have to say You did *jaw-dropping* work there. For which I bow in thanks. And so: amen.

Prayer for My Lovely Bride of Twenty-Seven Years

May you always be as vibrant and gracious and tender as you are today. May you never again in this blessed lifetime put milk on to heat for your coffee and turn the burner on high and wander away and get absorbed in something else and have to shriek and sprint into the kitchen as you have every! single! morning! since I met you thirty years ago. May you always be as selflessly engaged and fascinated by other people and unabsorbed by yourself as you are today. May you never again lie awake sleepless worrying that the children's struggles are totally your fault because you were not a good enough mom. May you always have those arresting blue-gray eyes exactly the color and potential fury of the sea. May you always be as graciously and kindheartedly and un-greedily you as you are today. May you someday love yourself as much as I love you. May you, when you finally pass into the next life at age 114, still looking like you are maybe thirty-seven, get total extra credit from the Merciful One for having cheerfully endured marriage to me for so long, though there were endless better candidates for husbandry, handsomer and richer and much more willing to go camping in the muddy sticky insect-ridden wilderness; but, trust me, none of them would have savored and appreciated and celebrated you as much as me. And so: amen.

Prayer for a Friend Finishing the Writing of a Difficult & Amazing Book in a Last Rush of Tiny Edits & Harried Rewrites & Epiphanies

For joy here at the end of the road. For peace of soul that you did the very best you could over many months of hard and arduous work, that you used your astounding tools to bring some light and sight to the readers and not incidentally to yourself. For a long sigh of workmanlike pleasure the week after you ship the book off to the press and file all your notes and clean your desk and wave good-bye, not with a tinge of sadness, to the adventure that was this combination of your curiosity and your heart and your itch to catch and tell stories that matter. For two days of sleeping late because by God you earned it. For the lowest of expectations for money and awards and the highest of expectations for connection to the heads and hearts of readers. For a blessing coming to you unexpectedly sometime soon that you will, with a growing smile, realize is a salute from the Author of All in celebration of how you milled your gifts into something that will last hundreds of years, if the publisher is wise and diligent. For a steaming delicious cup of tea on your porch after you walk back from the post office, and for a lazy hour in the sunlight, during which for a moment you start to think of all the parts of the book you could have made better, and then burst out laughing and realize the ship has sailed, and you wish it well, and all manner of things will be well. And for your next book, which will begin to niggle at your consciousness in about three months, mark my words. And so: amen.

Prayer Before Boarding a Flight

O, Lord, be merciful and let the plane get off the ground, and let it land without undue bumpage and rocking like that last flight at the end of which I thought I was going to have to collect my spinal vertebrae in a small bag and ooze my way off the jet. Let us be kind to the flight attendants, and not treat them as servants and lackeys, and berate them for things over which they have no control, like gate assignments and insipid flight entertainment. Keep the pilots in Your hand and ease their hangovers and romantic troubles, and remind them gently of their pride in their difficult craft. Enclose the poor girl hacking and coughing and making horrifying nasal sounds in an impervious bubble of air so that she does not infect the rest of us with her flu symptoms, especially this howling tiny baby next to me. Lend Your peace and strength to this child's mother so that she will be able to calmly corral the three-year-old terror even as she wears the tiny infant on her chest and must eventually grapple with large and intricate baggage. Lend this flight two or three of those cool large strong guys who smilingly get everyone's bags down from the overhead compartment as if the bags weighed ounces. Let us arrive safely and arrive home in the hearts of those

we love. Consider that the human creativity and inge-
nuity that made this airplane and flies it miraculously
is in a real sense a subtle prayer; for You allowed us
life, You allowed us the chance to rise to creativity, and
in Your mercy and love we may yet make You proud.
And so: amen.

Prayer to Saint Anthony of Padua

Sir, we hardly know each other, but I carry your face in my pocket, and often, if you will excuse the familiarity, I rub the medallion with your face on it with my thumb and forefinger, as some odd form of prayer or meditation during meetings, or while speaking in public, or while waiting not very patiently at the Department of Motor Vehicles, or in line at the library, or while standing with my heart in my mouth at the hospital, waiting for news; and I hope you know that I have great admiration for you, for your humility, for your eloquence when asked to speak of things that mattered, and because of the legend that you liked to talk to fish, who liked to listen to you and gathered in their multitudes for the event, which must have been a wonderful thing to see; so I hope that you will look kindly on us your successors among people trying fitfully to be humble and eloquent about things that matter, even if we do not talk to fish as much as perhaps we should. And so: amen.

Prayer for a Daughter Who Is Very Ill

Dear Coherent Mercy: I have a huge favor to ask. You will say, and rightly so, who am I to ask, me being such a muddle along the spiritual road; and I answer You forthrightly when I say I am a father, just like You, and I beg You to heal my daughter, I beg You to fill her with grace as you would fill a dry jar with water, for she is desiccated and bereft, she is despairing and dark, she is empty of hope and I am terrified for her health and sanity and future; such a bright wry child, such a witty patient teenager, and now she is greatly afflicted, and I stand before You and nakedly beg, with tears in my eyes and beseeching in my mouth; for You are a father too, and You know the bone-deep sadness of a father who can do nothing except worry and pray, and lie abed sleepless at night; so it is that here in the deep reaches of the night I come to You. Please, please, please—reach for her, cup her close, lift her winter, let her be born anew. Please. And so: amen.

Grinning Prayer at the Gentle Arrogance & Foolishness of Saying That There Are Only Five Forms of Catholic Prayer

With total respect for Adoration, Expiation, Love, Petition, and Thanksgiving, and with real affection for the earnest and genuine and diligent souls who arrived at this interesting organizational principle, the very idea of there being only five forms of prayer makes me laugh so hard I think I sprained an eyeball. There are as many forms of prayer as there have ever been hearts desperate to speak of longing and mercy and celebration and pleading. There are as many forms of prayer as all the words ever spoken by all the people who ever lived. There are as many forms of prayer as there have ever been beings of all species on the earth. Everything alive is a prayer. Your next breath is a prayer. Even your death will be a prayer, your last in the language of this body. There are no forms. Forms are only ways for us to try to grapple with That whom we cannot understand. Forms are very small things. We pray by being. This writing is a prayer. These fingers are praying. Laughing as we admit cheerfully we are silly and small and You are vast beyond measure and composed of love, that is a prayer. We will try to pray it all day today. And so: amen.

Prayer for People Whose Dads Left Them as Kids

Brothers and sisters, I have met some of you, and I admire the way you built yourself a self to live in since that awful wounding day and week and month and year; a year that never did end, did it? And I admire how you tell me what happened with a smile, as if you are way past it. I forbear to speak for my dad is a dear friend who never left me and is my hero to this day, and if I could share his gentle grace and wry humor and calm humility with you I would do so. I bow in sadness at the hole in your heart. I bow in quiet prayer for your poor lost father, who no matter what his excuse and defenses and idiocies must have spent at least some sleepless hours mulling his sins. I admire how every one of you I have met are intent on being good dads and mothers, sometimes to the point of being ferocious and maddening to your children, even as they understand why you are so intense. For your pain, my prayers. For some semblance of calm and acceptance of your father's sins, my prayers. In thanks that the Father abandons none of us, prayers. And so: amen.

Prayer of Thanks for Bass Players in Bands

Sisters and brothers, I see you, standing in the background by the stage curtain, diligent and anonymous. I hear your steady thrumming lines. I admire the consistency and little filigrees that you throw in to amuse the drummer, not that the self-absorbed guitarist or the vainglorious singer would ever notice. I hear the way your work drives the music and plants it deep in the roar of our hearts. I admire the brevity of your solo, granted you begrudgingly so that you do not whimper and shriek and snarl in rehearsals. I admire the epic height of your stand-up bass and the deep boom of your electric bass. I admire your general lack of pretension and ego. I admire the way you work without showing off. I wish we were all more like you and less like the preening naked walking ego that is your singer. I ask the blessing of the Manager of All Bands on your fingers and your soul; and thank the One for music, the greatest of all arts. And so: amen.

Prayer for Women Who Endured Abortions

Sisters, I stand before you without homily or lecture or opinion. I stand here naked on the page. I stand here with my hands extended in helpless prayer. I will never know your pain. I will never know your agony of spirit. I will never know the dark nights of your souls. I will never know the grinding fury of being lectured constantly by men who will never know what and how you felt. I stand here with only prayers in my mouth, for your peace, for the souls of the lost children, for the agony of your spirits and theirs. I have no wisdom. I have no stance or position or agenda. I leave all that outside the door. I only wish to reach for you and hold your hands and say I beg the love of the Unimaginable One on you and your lost children. There is a holy country beyond politics and religion and money and I want to stand there for a moment with you, even if it is just this one moment on this one page. My prayers for you and yours; may you meet again someday, and reach for each other, and find an eternity of peace and joy, in the light of the Love. And so: amen.

Prayer for Editors

Brothers and sisters, we are right in all decisions, and correct in all judgments, and bountiful in the sharing of our capacious wisdom. We catch the stories that must be told and attend brilliantly to the manner of their telling. We soothe the bruised egos of the poor childish writers who besiege us, and we gently teach our publishers how to ever serve us better with adulation and cash. We remain cheerfully humble even as we know how glorious and necessary we are, for a world without editors would be a mishmash of insipidity and muddle, lies and sales pitches, cliché and fatuity, naught but a storm of hollow wind. A prayer for us, then, brothers and sisters, that we remain humble, even as we are ever more necessary, and indeed the calm and surprisingly attractive saviors of civilization as we know it; for should we ever lose our humility, then we are as mere television anchors, mouthing stories that do not matter, and God help such a world. Onward, companions; but let us pause here for a moment, red pens in hand, and ask the blessings and graces of the Publisher of all things. And so: amen.

Last Prayer

Dear Coherent Mercy: thanks. Best life *ever*. Personally I never thought a cool woman would come *close* to understanding me, let alone understanding me but liking me anyway, but that happened! And You and I both remember that doctor in Boston saying polite but businesslike that we would not have children *but then came three children fast and furious!* And no man ever had better friends, and no man ever had a happier childhood and wilder brothers and a sweeter sister, and I was that rare guy who not only loved but *liked* his parents and loved sitting and drinking tea and listening to them! And You let me write some books that weren't half bad, and I got to have a career that actually no kidding helped some kids wake up to their best selves, and no one ever laughed more at the ocean of hilarious things in this world, or gaped more in astonishment at the wealth of miracles everywhere every moment. I could complain a little right here about the long years of back pain and the occasional awful heartbreak, but Lord, those things were infinitesimal against the slather of gifts You gave mere me, a muddle of a man, so often selfish and small. But no man was *ever* more grateful for Your profligate generosity, and here at the very end, here in my last lines, I close my eyes and weep with joy that I was *alive,* and blessed beyond measure, and might well be headed back home to the incomprehensible Love from which I came, mewling, many years ago. But hey, listen, can I ask one last favor? If I am sent back for another life, can I meet my lovely bride again? In whatever form? Could we be hawks, or otters maybe? And can we have the same kids again if possible? And if I get one friend again, can I have my buddy Pete? He was a huge guy in this life—make him the biggest otter ever, and I'll know him right away, okay? Thanks, Boss. Thanks from the bottom of my heart. See You soon. Remember—otters. Otters *rule*. And so: amen.

Brian Doyle is the editor of *Portland Magazine* at the University of Portland in Oregon—the finest spiritual magazine in America, says Annie Dillard. Doyle is the author of several books of essays, stories, "proems," nonfiction (notably *The Wet Engine*, about the "muddles & musics of the heart"), and fiction (notably the adventuresome novels *Mink River* and *The Plover*).

Doyle's work has appeared in *Atlantic Monthly*, *Harper's*, *Orion*, the *American Scholar*, the *Sun*, *Georgia Review*, and in newspapers and magazines around the world, including the *New York Times*, the *Times of London*, and the *Age* (in Australia). His essays have also been reprinted in the annual *Best American Essays*, *Best American Science & Nature Writing*, and *Best American Spiritual Writing* anthologies. Among various honors for his work is the Christopher Medal, a Catholic Book Award, the University of Notre Dame's Griffin Award in literature, three Pushcart Prizes, the John Burroughs Award for Nature Essays, the Foreword Reviews Novel of the Year award, and—puzzling him to this day—the Award in Literature from the American Academy of Arts and Letters. He is a regular contributor to a wide array of spiritual periodicals, among them *Commonweal*, *America*, *Notre Dame*, *Boston College*, *US Catholic*, the *Christian Century*, *Saint Anthony Messenger*, *National Catholic Reporter*, *First Things*, *Eureka Street* (in Australia), *Reality* (in Ireland), and *Give Us This Day*.

AVE

AVE MARIA PRESS

Founded in 1865, Ave Maria Press,
a ministry of the Congregation of
Holy Cross, is a Catholic publishing
company that serves the spiritual and
formative needs of the Church and its
schools, institutions, and ministers;
Christian individuals and families; and
others seeking spiritual nourishment.

For a complete listing of titles from

Ave Maria Press

Sorin Books

Forest of Peace

Christian Classics

visit www.avemariapress.com

AVE | AVE MARIA PRESS
Notre Dame, IN

A Ministry of the United States Province of Holy Cross